Copyright © 2011 by Alison Boyd Rasmussen

Published by The Fashion Doll Review

All rights reserved. No part of this book may be reproduced in any form without the author's written permission except in the case of brief quotations in critical articles and reviews. For more information contact the editor of the Fashion Doll Review at alison@fashiondollreview.com, or www.fashiondollreview.com.

edited by Melissa Metheney

ISBN: 0983681600
ISBN-13: 978-0-9836816-0-1

Ball-Jointed Dolls for Beginners

Finding the Doll of Your Dreams

by Alison Rasmussen of the Fashion Doll Review

edited by Melissa Metheney

Dedication

Special thanks to Peak's Woods, whose beautiful ball-jointed dolls are showcased in this book. I'm thrilled this company has given me permission to use their beautifully sculpted and wonderfully painted works of art in my photography.

Extra special thanks to Jen Eugley of JennyGrey Designs, for all the doll outfits used in this book. You can find more of her outfits for many dolls, including Tonner Dolls and Ellowyne Wilde, in her Etsy store at jennygrey.etsy.com. She takes commissions, too.

Warm wishes are extended to Ms. Cholong, the US representative for DollHeart, who has granted me permission to use their wonderful fashions in my photographs as well. Many of these outfits are perfectly sized for Peak's Woods bodies, as well as other dolls.

I'd also like to extend my thanks to Jacquie Biscardi (Sylphide) of GingerLime Designs, and Katie Brown (http://manoir-chaumont.livejournal.com) from Den of Angels for their lovely designs, which are also featured.

Thanks to Melissa Metheney, who has taken time out of her schedule to help me finish this project, edit this mess while it was still a pile of steaming you-know-what, and take out all of the poor little commas who were hoping to be printed. You are much appreciated.

A special secret thanks to Kathie Tilton, Carolyn Mitrovitch, and Valerie Sangster. You've given me more encouragement than you know, and you've convinced me that I do indeed have something worthwhile to share. I've been blessed by your friendship.

To the rest of the "fun" doll group and IFDC crowd--thanks for your encouragement. I love you guys!

To my family, hugs and kisses are due. David, you have been a huge help to me. Jake, I know you say you don't like dolls, but I love your enthusiasm just the same. Lauren, I love your encouragement. Kate, I love the evenings we've spent redressing our dolls together.

To Mark, my love: I've needed your encouragement for a long time. Thank you for your patience with me, your help around the house, and especially for Lavin. I couldn't have finished without you. I love you.

To the readers of the Fashion Doll Review: I hope this book can live up to your expectations. Thanks for your dedication over the past three years. Here's to many more to come!

Ball-Jointed Dolls for Beginners — 2
How to use this book — 3
Questions? — 4
What is a BJD? — 5
A brief history of the BJD — 7
My take on the Resin versus Vinyl debate — 8
Notes on sizes — 9
Commonly used terms and abbreviations — 11
Purchasing basics — 17
How collecting ball-jointed dolls is different from other types of collecting — 19
Words of caution — 21
Choosing your BJD — 23
Aesthetics: what's important to you — 24
Pricing and quality — 37
Themes and customization — 40
Notes about yellowing — 42
Purchasing your BJD — 43
To consider before your purchase — 44
In person — 49
Online — 50
On the secondary market — 52
Caring for your BJD — 55
BJD supplies — 56
Regular maintenance — 60
Basic customizing — 73
Restringing — 77
Enhancing projects — 89
Joining the BJD Community — 105
Netiquette — 107
Making online connections — 109
Meeting BJD collectors in person — 121
BJD resources — 125
Photo credits — 127
Doll emergencies — 129
Index — 131

Ball-Jointed Dolls for Beginners

Welcome to the wonderful world of ball-jointed dolls. Handmade, hand-painted, customized works of art, these dolls are the ultimate collector's plaything. Whether you are a new or experienced collector, this book is designed as a visual guide to your journey.

Most information you need about BJDs is available online, but it's hard to find and often inaccurate. While online message forums (such as Den of Angels) and blogs (The Fashion Doll Review and BJD Collectasy, for example) are helpful resources, it is time-consuming to find everything you need to know--not to mention intimidating.

Once you read through this book, however, you will know:

• the basic history of ball-jointed dolls and why they have become so popular

• how to budget for your collection and choose your design aesthetic

• how to order a doll and what prices and delivery times to expect

• how to take care of your doll, including everything from restringing to body blushing

• how connect to the BJD community, online and in person

• where to find additional resources

• which dolls, outfits, wigs, and eyes were used in each photo in this book.

I have experience in doll collecting--with making costly mistakes with my original collection--which I hope to share with you here in a humorous and user-friendly way, so you don't have to make the same ones.

Welcome to your journey! If you're on the fence about ball-jointed dolls, I hope this book will persuade you to take the leap.

How to use this book

Need instructions on how to read this book? Not really! However, there are several ways you can use it.

First, you may read it cover to cover. If you are a beginning BJD collector and you need to know the basics about ball-jointed dolls, that's your best bet.

Second, you might use this book as a reference. Use the **Index** as your guide to what you'd like to know. I've tried to include the terms, techniques, and definitions a BJD collector would want to find.

Third, you can use the **Table of Contents** to find what you need.

About my color-coded system:

- The green-edged pages signify the start of a new section.
- The purple-edged pages signify table references, which include lists of companies, definitions and so forth.
- The yellow boxes are simple *Do* and *Don't* tips, which you may read or ignore.

Fourth, if you need help with your doll--including everything from changing your doll's wig to restringing and sanding--turn to the section labeled **How to care for your BJD**. I'll go over many techniques, as well as little tips and tricks I've learned over the years.

Fifth, if you are having budgeting problems with your doll collection, I highly recommend reading through this book in its entirety. I'm no budgeting genius, as my dear husband can tell you. However, I do have some techniques to help you plan your collection, and how to stick to any dollar amount you wish. I address budgeting specifically in **What is a BJD** and **How to choose your BJD**.

Finally, if you are looking for a specific Peak's Woods sculpt--and I only use Peak's Woods dolls in this book--look up her name in the **Index**. I've listed the pages in which each doll's photo appears, next to her sculpt name.

Questions?

Like what you see here? You can friend me on Den of Angels or Flickr. You can find links to all my online information on my blog, The Fashion Doll Review, or our Facebook fan page.

Visit www.BJDsForBeginners.com for all the links you find in this book, special information about the models used, and other information. I'm more than happy to answer any or all of your questions.

My user name on Den of Angels, the Resin Café, Zone of Zen, and the American BJD Forum is **alington**. Feel free to "friend" me on those message forums.

Please feel free to contact me via email, also, at alison@bjdsforbeginners.com. I'd love to hear from you!

What is a BJD?

A ball-jointed doll, as I refer to it in this book, is an articulated doll with ball and socket joints. The dolls are intended for adult collectors, look realistic and pose very well.

They are strung with elastic, usually in two loops: the first through the torso, from the right wrist to the left. The second is looped twice through the length of the body (secured with a metal hook at the neck), and down each leg, hooking at the ankle joints.

Ball-jointed dolls are usually made of polyurethane synthetic resin, which is a hard plastic that is poured into molds. This is a brittle plastic, and has rough, sharp edges when first cast, so the doll may need to be sanded (especially the seams, or the parting lines) either by the owner or the manufacturer.

Do get used to the BJD jargon and terms used in this book. Refer to pages 12-16 for more information.

The dolls are usually fairly realistically proportioned--in comparison to fashion dolls, at least--and have realistically sized feet, which allow them to stand on their own. They also are usually anatomically correct. Fantasy dolls are widely available, with fairy wings, goats' hooves, mermaid tails, as well as a variety of fantasy horns, ears, tails and more. Sometimes these fantasy parts are held to a normal body with magnets, or are strung to the doll in place of human limbs.

The faces of BJDs are painted by hand or with an airbrush, allowing them to have an individual, incredibly realistic look. BJDs are wigged and have hair that is easily changed. Eyes are acrylic, glass, or silicone, and can be changed by removing the head cap and replacing the eye putty which holds them in place.

A single BJD can have many different looks. Your ball-jointed doll is one-of-a-kind, made just for you, usually upon order. Your BJD's unique joints, sculpting and eyes allow her to adopt human-like poses and expressions, unlike other kinds of dolls.

A brief history of the BJD

While the creation of porcelain dolls with ball and socket joints is traditional in the doll-making world, the ball-jointed doll as we know it is a recent phenomenon. Volks, a Japanese hobby company, first introduced the Super Dollfie in 1999. Its sculptor was Akihiro Enku, and their first doll was 57 cm tall. The doll was introduced as a "garage kit" and sold in parts for the new owner to customize, paint, and assemble. By 2003, the garage kit style had faded to the fully assembled, limited edition full-set doll we know today. Volks was originally trying to create a product marketed toward female customers with the production of Super Dollfie.

By 2002, South Korean companies like Custom House and Cerberus Project jumped into the market to compete. Today, some of the most beloved BJD companies are from the area, such as Soom, Doll in Mind, Fairyland and my personal favorite, Peak's Woods.

Since 2005, China has stepped up to the competition as well, with its own original companies and sculpting style, such as Dollzone, Bobobie, and others.

Goodreau Doll was the first American company to produce a BJD in 2007, followed by Berdine Creedy and Kim Lasher.

Unfortunately, it is as easy now as it was then to find plaster or low-quality resin knock-offs. Take care when you find unusually low-priced bargain dolls on eBay. Recast dolls are *not* the real thing and may damage easily. They are a copyright infringement on the original artist's sculpt and are banned from online communities as bootlegs. Subscribe to Yve's blog, http://freakylittledolls.blogspot.com, for a reliable source of information on copied dolls.

My take on the *Resin versus Vinyl* debate

In the community of BJD collectors, there is an ongoing discussion on the issue of resin versus vinyl. "Is my doll a BJD if it's vinyl?"

Well, in my opinion--and I'm just a single collector--this is a question of semantics. If your doll has ball and socket joints, it's strung with elastic, *and* it's vinyl--then yes. I would say, sure! It's a ball-jointed doll.

There are other fashion dolls on the market made from vinyl with mechanical (not strung) ball and socket joints. These are not technically BJDs. Plus, consider the many resin fashion dolls on the market: Sybarites, Tonner Doll's BJDs, JamieShow, Doug James, Numina, and others. Some are even created by BJD companies, such as Dollmore's FMD (Fashion Model Doll), whose 12" model can share clothes with Barbie and Fashion Royalty dolls. What about those dolls? Why aren't they included in the ball-jointed doll category?

Why does it even matter?

Well, first, you'll want to be aware of which dolls are on-topic at various online groups, message boards and forums, and your local doll club. You probably don't want to call a fashion doll a ball-jointed doll when she isn't one. You don't want to offend anyone who isn't related to you.

Second, it's important to know the difference between resin and vinyl. This is why:

- Vinyl stains more easily than resin. When resin stains from dark clothing, you can remove the stain with Magic Eraser without harming the doll or scratching. Vinyl stains are harder to remove.

- Vinyl has a different feel and smell to it than resin. It's lighter than resin. It's more flexible than resin. Resin can be sanded without scratching. Resin luminesces in photos.

- Vinyl is harder to paint and less forgiving than resin. You can use chalk pastels and sealer on resin.

***Don't** be afraid of your new ball-jointed beauty! There's almost nothing you can do to her that can't be fixed!*

While vinyl might seem a better, sturdier choice for a doll--and it is, for a child's doll, I'm sure!--I have to confess, I am smitten with resin.

New BJD collectors should not be afraid of the so-called fragility of resin. If you drop any doll on a tile floor, chances are something will break. Resin is much sturdier than porcelain, and it stains less easily than vinyl. You can easily remove stains with Magic Eraser, which makes it easier to dress your BJD in one-of-a-kind (OOAK) clothing (for which fabric stains might be a concern).

If you have super-glue on hand, you should be fine in case of breakage. Additionally, you can order replacement hands or feet (fingers and resin hooks seem to be the most common breaking points) directly from the manufacturer.

Notes on sizes

Ball-jointed dolls are classified into three size groups: large dolls, mini dolls, and tiny dolls.

Large dolls

Large dolls range from 50 cm (19.5") and over, averaging about 60 cm (20.5") or about 1/3 scale. Some measure up to 90 cm (35.5") tall.

Volks' name for this size of doll is "Super Dollfie," or SD, which many companies and collectors use freely. The numbers that often follow this term (SD10, SD13, SD16) are Volks' unique sizing system and designate particular doll measurements. You can see them on their website (www.volksusa.com). Other companies have their own names for this size of doll; for instance, Peak's Woods calls this size FOC (Fairy of Color).

Mini dolls

Mini dolls range from 30-50 cm (11.75"-19.5"). There are two types in this category: dolls that are meant to look like younger siblings or children of the 1/3 scale dolls, and slim minis, who are mature, 1/4 scale dolls.

Volks' name for this size is "Mini Super Dollfie," or MSD. Peak's Woods calls this size FOB (Fairy of Bugs).

Tiny dolls

These are any dolls under 30 cm (11.75"). There are many sizes of these, too.

Volks YoSD size, Peak's Woods' FOF (Fairy of Fairytales), and Fairyland's LittleFee are about 27 cm (10.5") and are supposed to be a toddler size on the 1/3 scale.

You can also find 1/6 scale dolls about the size of Barbie, such as Mini Gem by Soom.

Even smaller dolls are available--Fairyland makes a Real Puki size that is only 9.5 cm (3.75") tall--perfect for a pocket-size doll.

Commonly used terms and abbreviations

For your reference, here is a list of commonly used terms and abbreviations you might see online and in the BJD community and in this book.

Do take the time to learn the terminology. It's OK to look like a n00b, but remember: it's a fine line between n00b and b00b.

BJD-specific terms

Term	Extended	Definition
ABJD	Asian ball-jointed doll	a BJD with Asian "aesthetics." More on this later.
AIL	Alice in Labyrinth	a Japanese doll manufacturer
AoD	Angel of Dream	a Chinese doll manufacturer
AR	Neo Angel Region	a Korean doll manufacturer
AS	Angell Studio	a Chinese doll manufacturer
B&G	Boy and Girl	a Chinese doll manufacturer
BBB	Bobobie	a Chinese doll manufacturer, sister company of Resinsoul
BC	Bambicrony	a Korean doll manufacturer
Beautiful White		Fairyland's term for white skin
BF	Blue Fairy	a Korean doll manufacturer
BJD	ball-jointed doll	
blushing	sometimes referred to as brushing	adding color to your doll's body with pastels or an airbrush
BUMP	Bring Up My Post	In forums, BUMP-ing your post means adding a comment to your own post and bringing it to the top of the discussion. Many forums don't allow this.
BW	Beauty White	Volks' term for white skin (also known as Snow Skin)
Catish		a line of dolls from Dollmore
CH	Custom House	a Korean doll manufacturer
COA	certificate of authenticity	paperwork, provided by the BJD's manufacturer, stating the doll's name, sculpt and date of production
Con	convention	
Cosplay	Costume Play	dressing up as your favorite anime or video-game character
CP	Cerebus Project	an older Korean BJD company, which now sculpts for Luts and Fairyland
crazy legs		when your doll has trouble sitting or standing, due to too tight or too loose stringing
DD	Dollfie Dream	Volks' vinyl doll line, 60cm tall
DDE	Denver Doll Emporium	a BJD and fashion doll dealer, which sells dolls, wigs, eyes and more
DH	DollHeart	a Chinese manufacturer of doll clothing
DIM	Doll in Mind	a Korean doll manufacturer
DK	Dolkot	a Korean doll manufacturer
DM	Dollmore	a Chinese doll manufacturer
DoA	Den of Angels	the largest English-speaking BJD online message forum
DoD	Dream of Doll	a Korean doll manufacturer
DoD	Dust of Dolls	a French doll manufacturer
Dollfie		A term often incorrectly used instead of "BJD." Dollfie really is Volks' term for its 1/6 scale vinyl models.
DollnDoll		a Korean doll manufacturer and online doll reseller
Dollshe		a Korean doll manufacturer
DOLPA	Doll Party	doll parties hosted by Volks, in which you can find ultra limited edition BJDs and outfits
double-jointed		refers to an elbow or knee joint with a third part, which allows for increased mobility in that limb
dreaming		sculpt in which the eyes are a little bit open

Term	Extended	Definition
DT	Dollstown	a Korean doll manufacturer
DZ	Dollzone	a Chinese doll manufacturer
ED	Enchanted Doll	doll eye manufacturer, and also a porcelain OOAK doll artist in Canada
Elfdoll		a Korean doll manufacturer, which uses sculpts created by Rainman
EMS	Express Mail Service	In the US, this is Global Express Mail.
F01-F21		head sculpts by Volks, used in the Full Choice System
face-up		refers to your doll's face paint
FCS	Full Choice System	offered by Volks to create your own doll
Fdoll	Fantasy Doll	a Chinese doll manufacturer
feeler		If you're thinking of selling or buying a doll, but haven't decided, you can post a "feeler" first. Many forums don't allow this.
Fer		Type of outfit (long ruffled dress with a hooded, long ruffled cape) manufacturer by DollHeart. Some companies sell exclusively colored or sized Fers, created by DH.
FOB	Fairy of Bugs	the 42 cm line of dolls from Peak's Woods
FOC	Fairy of Color	the 58 cm line of dolls from Peak's Woods
FOF	Fairy of Fairies	the 27 cm line of dolls from Peak's Woods
Forever Dolls		a Chinese doll manufacturer, no longer in business, as its dolls were poor, unauthorized reproductions of Volks head sculpts
FP	face plate	Some BJDs, like Fairyland, Kaye Wiggs and U-Noa, have interchangeable face plates that can be removed from the front, instead of a removable head cap.
French resin		Polyurethane resin with a translucent glow, which is both more difficult and more expensive to pour, and unfortunately, may yellow more quickly than opaque resins.
Hound		A doll by Dollshe, taller than most BJDs at about 70 cm
IH	Iplehouse	a Korean doll manufacturer
IoS	Immortality of Soul	a Korean doll manufacturer
JID	Junior Iplehouse Doll	a line of dolls from Iplehouse
Large BJDs		Generally, these are dolls that stand taller than 50 cm.
LB	large bust	An option for your doll--some companies allow you to add an additional "+ large" option when you place your order. You'll receive an additional torso piece with the doll you ordered, poured at the same time.
LD	Latidoll	a Korean doll manufacturer
LE	limited edition	a limited edition run of dolls, either limited to a specific edition size or limited to a certain ordering period
Leekeworld		a Korean doll manufacturer, known for its wigs
Limhwa		a Korean doll manufacturer
limited face-up		special make-up, limited to an event doll
LSG	light slate gray	color of resin used to pour a doll, specific to Bambicrony
LTF	Little Fee	The "Yo" size of doll from Fairyland, a Korean doll manufacturer
Luts		a Korean doll manufacturer
Mini BJDs		These dolls range between 30-50 cm. They can be younger siblings of large dolls, or they can be miniature adults.

Term	Extended	Definition
MNF	Mini Fee	line of adult-bodied mini dolls, once available through Cerberus Project, now sold through Fairyland
MoC	Mint on Card	an online doll shop and BJD dealer
modding		making permanent changes to the BJD's sculpt--changing the size/shape of eye sockets, ears, lips, etc.
model body		This size of doll is usually taller than 58-60 cm dolls, and is usually more shapely than girlish.
Model doll		taller girl, originally available only from Dollmore
MP	Masterpiece	soft-glass eye company
MSC	Mr. Super Clear	spray-on coating to prevent staining and yellowing on resin, plus great for face-up/blushing primer. Available in matte and UV-cut.
MSD	Mini Super Dollfie	Volks' term for mini BJDs, but some companies "borrow" this term for dolls within the 30-42 cm range.
Narin		a Korean doll manufacturer
NB	normal bust	An option for your doll. This may be a girl-sized bust on an MSD-sized doll.
Nobility Doll		a Korean doll manufacturer
Notdoll		a Korean doll manufacturer
NS	normal skin	color of resin used to pour a doll
PF	Pocket Fairy	doll line made by Blue Fairy
PKF	PukiFee	a line of dolls from Fairyland
pureskin		Volks current resin color
PW	Peak's Woods	a Korean doll manufacturer
RD	Rainy Doll	a line of dolls from Elfdoll
restringing		when you replace the elastic cording inside your BJD to improve posing or because of wear
Ringdoll		a Chinese doll manufacturer
RS	Resinsoul	a Chinese doll manufacturer, sister company of Bobobie
sanding		smoothing out seam lines or nicks from the BJD's body
SD	Super Dollfie	Volks' term for large BJDs, but some BJD companies "borrow" this term for dolls ranging from 50-65 cm.
SD10		Volks body type
SD13		Volks body type
SD16		Volks body type
Secret Doll		a Korean doll manufacturer
SID	Senior Iplehouse Doll	a line of dolls from Iplehouse
sleeping		sculpt in which the eyes are completely shut
Soom		a Korean doll manufacturer, maker of lots of fantasy dolls
Souldoll		a Korean doll manufacturer
stringing		refers to the elastic cording inside your BJDs body
sueding		adding microsuede (or hot glue) to the inside of your BJD's joints to improve your doll's posing ability
Swarrico		A child's sitting pose, in which both legs are turned out. Some BJDs have L shaped slots in them, so their thighs can rotate in toward each other.
tan		color of resin used to pour a doll, usually costs more than white or normal to pour because of color matching issues.

Term	Extended	Definition
Tender		sculpt in which the eyes are half-closed
Testors DC	Testors Dullcote	an alternative spray to Mr. Superclear, which can be found at hobby and craft stores
Tiny BJDs		These dolls are smaller 30 cm. They can be children, or young tiny adults (or fairies).
U-Noa		a line of dolls created by the Japanese company Alchemic Lab
UD	Unidoll	a Korean doll manufacturer
UFK	unfinished kit	BJD which comes in a kit for you to finish, paint and put together
urethane resin		this is the traditional opaque resin poured in molds to make BJDs
UV coating		spraying your doll with Mr. Superclear UV coat to protect your doll from premature yellowing
Volks		a Japanese doll manufacturer
wake-up		sculpt in which the eyes are about half-open
wiring		adding wire to the elastic canals in your doll to assist in holding a pose. I don't recommend this, as wire often wears down the resin inside joints and canals. Instead, use proper stringing and sueding to help your doll pose. Or with tiny dolls, you can use pipe cleaners to protect the resin.
WS	white skin	color of resin used to pour a doll
yellowing		the process of resin slowly changing to a yellow hue as a result of exposure to light and environmental factors
Yo	YoSD	Another way to express the term, "YoSD": Volks' term for tiny BJDs, which some BJD companies "borrow" for dolls 27 cm and under.
YoSD		Volks' term for tiny BJDs, but some BJD companies "borrow" this term for dolls 27 cm and under.

Web-specific terms

Term	Extended	Definition
BIN	Buy It Now	a term from eBay, which allows the buyer to pay a set price for an auction instead of placing a bid.
Blogger	www.blogger.com	a free blogging website
DH	Dear Husband, Darling Husband	sometimes used facetiously
FA	for auction	used in for-sale posts
FM	Flickr Mail	Flickr's instant message system
FS	for sale	used in for-sale posts
HTH	hope that helps	
IIRC	if I remember correctly	
IM	instant message	
IMHO	in my humble opinion	
IMO	in my opinion	
IRL	in real life	usually refers to real-life dolls, as opposed to promotional photos
LF	looking for	used in want-to-buy posts
LJ	Live Journal	a free blogging website
LMAO	laughing my ass off	ROFLMAO can be used together
LOL	laugh out loud	
MIA	missing in action	
MIB	mint in box	used in for-sale posts
MOD	moderator	person who watches over the forum
N00B	pronounced "newb" for "newbie"	Someone who is new to the forum, group or hobby, someone who is less experienced.
NF	nothing further	used when you don't have any text in your message post and you've replied in the subject line only
NIB	new in box	used in for-sale posts
NRFB	never removed from box	used in for-sale posts
NSFW	not safe for work	used in photo posts
NTB	need to buy	used in want-to-buy posts
NWS	not work safe	used in photo posts
OBO	or best offer	used in for-sale posts
OOAK	one of a kind	
OOP	out of production	
OT	off topic	
PM	private message	
ROF	rolling on the floor	
TDF	to die for	
TLC	tender loving care	used for dolls that need work
WIP	work in progress	
WTB	want to buy	used in want-to-buy posts
WTC	want to commission	
WTF	whiskey tango foxtrot or what the f&*%?	
WTT	want to trade	
Y!	Yahoo	

Purchasing basics

Before purchasing your first BJD, you should know a few important things about them.

First, most of the mini (30-50 cm) and large dolls (50 cm and taller) are anatomically correct. If you're already collecting fashion dolls or action figures, this is an important fact to know to avoid any surprises. From what I've seen, these parts aren't sculpted in a gross way, but you'll want to consider this when choosing outfits and underclothing.

Second, when you purchase a "basic" doll, he or she will come nude or in underwear. Often, the doll will include a wig and eyes, but sometimes you'll need to purchase these separately.

Third, when you buy a BJD, you usually need to pay extra for a quality **face-up** (the doll's face painting--more on this in the next chapter). As in all things in life, you get what you pay for. Unless you plan to paint your doll yourself, make sure you've seen real-life owner photos of the company face-up (in addition to company promotional photos), so you know what to expect.

Fourth, you'll want to be sure you're dealing with a reputable company. Formerly reputable companies may be caught stealing another artist's idea or blatantly copying a sculpt. I don't know why this is so common in the BJD world, but it is. Look up the company in Den of Angels before placing your order.

Check the company's delivery times to make sure there aren't any backlogs. Keep in mind that around Chinese New Year (it's lunar, so it lands around the end of January or in February most years) most companies close for at least a week (if not an entire month), so you should expect a delay in processing and shipping.

Finally, check out owner photos and ask questions about how happy the owners are with the doll's quality and ability to hold a pose out of the box and so forth on Den of Angels, Flickr, Zone of Zen, the Resin Café, and anywhere you can find photos of your doll. You're making an investment. You want to be happy with your first doll!

I recommend doing all these things *before* you place your order.

> ***Do** take your time to do your homework. It's pretty much always a seller's market when it comes to BJDs.*

How collecting ball-jointed dolls is different from other types of collecting

I've been a doll collector since I was seven. I took a short and reluctant break in my teens and twenties, though I confess to walking through the toy aisle on a regular basis even then. Since the arrival of my first ball-jointed doll, however, my collection has been through several makeovers. Not only are ball-jointed dolls different than other types of dolls, but how I view my collection has changed.

How BJDs are different than other dolls

I collect vintage Barbies, in addition to pink box and contemporary ones, and I can see the value of having these dolls in pristine, never-removed-from-the-box condition. The age of the doll, wear, color, and styling--all the way down to the doll's smell--are what make the doll valuable.

When you remove the doll from her packaging, you decrease the doll's value instantly. You risk messing up her hair or smudging the delicate vinyl face with oil from your hands, and already you've exposed her to light damage and premature aging. The best way to shield these dolls from damage (and maintain their value) is to keep them in their boxes and shippers, away from light and dust.

Some fashion doll collectors redress and restyle their dolls--but you need to be careful unless you're skilled at hair repair, fixing tiny seams on clothing, and sewing on buttons and snaps. Playline items aren't built to last fifty years, and collector dolls aren't built for play.

But ball-jointed dolls are.

Your new BJD arrives to you blank--or nearly blank--with the expectation that you, her new owner, will give her a name, paint her face, and give her a character and style. She expects you to first build her into the "real girl" she is meant to be, and then be changed, over and over, until she fits whatever fantasy you want her to be. She's the ideal multi-faceted collector's plaything.

When I first encountered a real-life ball-jointed doll, she took my breath away. When I first discovered the aesthetic I loved the most--fantasy/anime inspired--my doll collection was in for a change. When my first Peak's Woods doll arrived at my door, my doll collection changed forever.

How my view of collecting has changed

Because I am now not only allowed, but *supposed* to redress, restyle, and change my dolls, my collection has become more personal and unique. It has taken some years to realize my design aesthetic and choose my ideal styling, but it has happened, and it's fun!

What a relief not to have to wait on a doll company to create the perfect doll and outfit combination anymore! *You* choose the doll of your dream, the eye color, the hair color, and the outfit you desire. Then, you can change it next week. It's nothing short of fantastic.

Or if you dare, add a friend--and have two to display similar styles or different ones! You'll be surprised how your collection grows and changes into a style that is uniquely yours.

There is no right way to build your collection. Only know that it's yours, and it reflects you and your own style. There may be dolls that are worth more in other collectors' eyes, but the dollar value doesn't matter if it doesn't reflect your own personal aesthetic.

I want to show you how to find your aesthetic, and narrow it down, so you can create your own perfect ball-jointed doll to start, or add to, your collection.

I've found that how I look at my dolls has become more fluid--I don't feel tied down to them, like I can't rearrange them or sell a doll I only sort of like. Why hang on to dolls you like when you can find a doll you truly *love*? This frees up your budget to view collecting in a whole new light. Not having to hold onto every doll I've ever purchased was a huge source of relief, and allowed for some funds to start my BJD collection.

Words of caution

Before we jump into the next section, I thought I'd take a minute to offer a few words of caution. When you start any new expensive hobby, you're bound to meet some resistance from friends and family.

Friends and family reactions to your new hobby

"You want to spend $300 on a *doll*?"

"Don't you have *enough* dolls already?"

"You're starting *another* collection?"

"Why spend so much money on a piece of plastic?"

Don't worry. Your feelings, dreams and new obsessions are perfectly normal. You're not going crazy.

Why, indeed? Plan to have at least a few members of your family and friends who won't be as excited about your new hobby as you are. Be prepared for some teasing, or worse.

If you're not particularly sensitive, this won't be a big deal for you. But for some people, this can be awful. In this case, you might consider why you got into the hobby in the first place: obsession, love of beauty, passion for fashion.

Myself, I see my ball-jointed beauties as one-of-a-kind works of art--similar to what others might hang on their walls--only I can enhance, manipulate, and fix up my collection; build them out of pieces and improve them; change them up and personalize them. It's social: I involve my daughters and friends in the hobby.

The money pit

Before you order your first doll, remember that collections are built up slowly. You don't have to spend all of your money at once, and you can plan out what you'd like to add as you go along. Don't slide down the slippery slope of a BJD-dedicated credit card. I'll get into budgeting in the next chapter.

Even a budget of $10 per week will be able to get you the BJD of your dreams--it will just take a little longer. Plus, you'll lose the risk of adding expensive dolls to your collection that you don't love, and end up appreciating what you have.

The All Night Obsession

Finally, be prepared for a few wakeful nights with this hobby. Like any new venture, you'll find yourself thinking about new ideas, projects, and characters for your dolls. I recommend a couple things to help, and for insomnia:

- Keep a notebook by your bed. It's handy, and you can write down any thoughts you have during the night. You won't lose them, and you can "safely" get some rest.

- Start a blog. This is a great way to keep track of project ideas, and it might even get you feedback and encouragement to get those projects started (and finished).

Now, let's move on to the next section, so we can find the perfect BJD for you!

Choosing your BJD

No, I won't actually tell you which doll to choose.

Well, maybe I will. I highly recommend purchasing a doll from Peak's Woods, which has graciously allowed me to use its dolls as models in my book. These girls have the perfect balance of articulation and joint attractiveness, and I haven't encountered a higher quality resin. Their facial sculpts are amazing, and face-up quality is fantastic. I'm a little embarrassed to admit how many of their dolls I own!

Additionally, you should choose an outfit from DollHeart, and commission another from JennyGrey Designs, as these companies have given me permission to use their outfits in my book.

You'll also find designs in this book created by Jacquie Biscardi of GingerLime Designs, and Katie Brown, of the Manoir Chaumont Live Journal blog, from Den of Angels. They have both graciously permitted me to use their lovely outfits in this book.

Do visit the websites of the artists and BJD companies featured in this book. They are true treasures!

Moving on, I'll help you determine what sort of aesthetics are important to you, as well as addressing pricing versus quality. Finally, I'll discuss customization options.

Aesthetics: what's important to you

Take another breath, dear Reader; take a step back before you plop down your first chunk of change.

When I bought my very first BJD, I thought long and hard before my first purchase. I searched everywhere--magazines, owner photos, and so on--to ensure I got the doll of my dreams. When I paid off Peak's Woods Sky on lay-away, I wasn't disappointed: she was everything I'd hoped for and more!

But I lost myself somewhere along the way. I bought bargain dolls, and dolls that weren't quite right, and I ended up with a bunch I liked, but didn't love. I ended up selling them later.

Part of the reason I'm writing this book is to help you avoid my costly mistakes, and to help you narrow down your style *before* you make your first investment.

It's possible you aren't an impulse shopper like I was. In that case, you'll do well. But many doll collectors are, however, and they don't do well in the BJD world. It's easy to get over your head, especially with limited edition dolls.

Let's begin by narrowing down some aesthetic styles--this book is filled with mine, for simplicity's sake--and end with staying organized. That will get you off to a brilliant start.

Asian versus American aesthetics

This is a complicated issue. Honestly, it comes down to a matter of taste. I believe each manufacturer has its own look about its dolls and sculpts. Some collectors believe that each country also has a certain look to its dolls, but I think the doll sculpts vary too much for that claim.

Basically, the way I understand it, the thought used to go like this: "American" sculpts are child-like and less realistic than "Asian" sculpts. "American" bodies have less range of motion than "Asian" bodies, and are sculpted with "tube-like" limbs. "American" sculpts aren't as detailed as "Asian" sculpts; therefore, we won't allow them on our message board or forum.

An important side note here that you'll hear me repeat: I do believe if independent people set up their own message board or forum, and you wish to participate, you must follow their rules. So keep this in mind if there is a particular message forum you'd like to join. It's only common courtesy that you follow the rules of the moderators on each message board you join. See the section on Netiquette (page 105) for more information.

Don't be offended if I state something a little controversial here. You don't have to agree with me, of course.

Now, my personal opinion on the aesthetic issue is that today, there is *little* difference between American and Asian BJD articulation, detailing, and quality. In fact, when you buy a doll from Goodreau, Berdine Creedy, or Kim Lasher, the seam lines are already sanded and the dolls stand up perfectly, right out of the box, no sueding required. The face-up is painted, the eyes are set, and everything you need is included (the outfit, shoes and wig). The resin is high quality and yellows very slowly and evenly. The dolls pose well, and some are now available double-jointed with attractive and realistic joints. You really get good-looking dolls from American sculptors, and I love them. I don't think American sculpts are in *any* way "inferior" to Asian sculpts--though I will state that each company's sculptor has a unique style of her own, and that may or may not suit your taste.

It's a matter of preference. I don't understand how Kaye Wiggs' sweet faces are included in the "on-topic" Asian sculpts and Kim Lasher's adorable little faces aren't. They look like they are in a similar aesthetic group to me.

This is just my opinion on the subject. Please take it or leave it, and buy the doll whose face you adore. Then find a discussion group in which he or she is on-topic. Or start your own, if you'd like!

Do *feel free to make your own opinion. I hope to help you develop your own style!*

Realistic versus exaggerated features

Now, let's get to what you like. First, decide which features you like most--do you prefer more realistic features on a doll's face, or more anime-inspired features? Do you like fantasy or human dolls?

This list will help show you what's available and help narrow down your choices. Many companies make both realistic and exaggerated sculpts. Hopefully this will you get started.

Just to be clear: Realistic means the head is proportioned like a real person, and the eyes are the right size. Exaggerated means the head or eyes might be larger than life.

Fantasy means the dolls are available with horns, wings, fins or hooves. These classifications are just my opinions--not everyone would agree with me on this list.

Don't feel like you have to agree with my stylistic opinions. The point is to get you to think about your own.

Company	Realistic	Exaggerated	Fantasy	Website
5StarDoll		X	X	http://www.5stardoll.com/
Alchemic Laboratory	X		X	http://www.alchemiclabo.com/
Alice In Labyrinth	X			http://ail-dolls.com/
Angel of Dream (AOD)		X	X	http://www.aoddoll.net/
Angel Street	X		X	http://www.angel-street.com/
Angel Toast		X	X	http://www.angeltoastdolls.com/store/
Angelheim	X		X	http://angelheim.com/
Angell Studio	X		X	http://www.angell-studio.com/en/
AngelsDoll	X			http://www.angelsdoll.net/
Another Secret	X	X		http://anothersecret7.blogbus.com/
AnotherSpace2		X		http://anotherspace2.com/index.php
ariPina	X			http://www.aripina.com/index.php
Asleep Eidolon	X	X		http://www.aedoll.cn/exhibition/root.asp?anid=1
Astral In Rainbow		X	X	http://jinsiwoo.namoweb.net/
Bambicrony		X	X	http://bambicrony.net/index.php
Berdine Creedy	X			http://www.netcollecting.com/
Bimong (Narin & Narae)	X		X	http://www.art-bimong.com/
Bishonen House	X		X	http://www.bishonenhouse.com/
Blue Blood Doll	X			http://www.blueblooddoll.com/
Blue Fairy	X	X	X	http://www.blueblooddoll.com/
Bo Bergemann BJD		X	X	http://www.bergemanndolls.com/
Bobobie	X		X	http://www.bobobie.com/
Boy&Girl (B&G) Dolls		X	X	http://www.ibgdoll.com/en/
Camellia Dynasty		X	X	http://www.camelliadynasty.com/
Castle Anne		X		http://castleanne.com/
Cherishdoll		X		http://www.cherishdoll.us/
Crobi Doll		X		http://crobidolls.com/
CutieAngel		X		http://ctangel.com/index.php
Dawn Donofrio Originals	X			http://www.dawndonofrio.com/gallery/
Dear Mine			X	http://www.dearminedoll.com/main/index.php
DikaDoll		X	X	http://www.dkdoll.com/abouten.asp
DIM (Doll in Mind)	X	X	X	http://www.dimdoll.com/
Distant Memory	X			http://distantmemory.net/main.htm
Dolkot		X		http://www.dolkot.com/
Doll Family – A	X	X	X	http://www.dfdoll-a.com/
Doll Family – H	X	X	X	http://www.dollfamily-h.com/fengtian/cn

Company	Realistic	Exaggerated	Fantasy	Website
Doll Leaves		X	X	http://www.doll-leaves.com/
Doll Stories		X		http://www.dollstories.com/
Doll-Love		X	X	http://www.doll-love.com/
DollFactory	X	X	X	http://edollfactory.com/
Dollmore	X	X	X	http://www.dollmore.net/
DollnDoll		X	X	http://www.dollndoll.com/
Dolls Town	X	X		http://dollstown.com/mydoll.htm
DollShe Craft	X			http://www.dollshecraft.com./
Dollstol		X		http://www.dollstol.com/src/main/indexpage.php
DollZone	X	X	X	http://www.doll-zone.com/
Domadoll	X	X		http://www.domadoll.com/
Domuya	X		X	http://www.domuya.net/
DragonDoll	X	X		http://dragondoll.com/en/
Dream of Doll		X	X	http://www.dreamofdoll.com/
DreamingDoll	X	X		http://ddollshop.com/
Elfdoll	X		X	http://dec66292.dreamweb.co.kr/index.php
Elysium doll	X	X		http://elysiumdoll.com/jpmain.htm
FairyGarden		X	X	http://www.dd-anne.com/
Fairyland	X	X	X	http://dollfairyland.com/
Fantasiation		X		http://www.fantasiation.com/BJD.htm
Fantasy Doll		X		http://www.fdoll.com/
Garden of Dolls		X	X	http://www.gardenofdolls.com/
Glorydoll	X		X	http://glorydoll.com/index.php
Goodreau Doll Lab	X	X	X	http://goodreaudollstore.com/
HTT Dolls		X		http://httdolls.webs.com/
Hypermaniac	X			http://hypermaniac.com/
I-Doll Studio	X			http://i-dollstudio.com/zbxe/main
Immortality of Soul	X		X	http://isis.dothome.co.kr/
ImpDoll		X		http://impdoll.com/
IMPLDoll	X	X	X	http://www.impldoll.com
Infiniti Doll		X		http://www.infinitidoll.com/
IpleHouse	X		X	http://www.iplehouse.net/
Island Doll		X	X	http://www.islanddoll.com/en/
ixtee (ixDOLL)		X		http://www.ixdoll.com/catalog/index.php
Jaime Doll		X	X	http://www.jaime-doll.net/
Jakzjewelz		X		http://www.jakzjewelz.com/
JAMIEshow	X		X	http://www.angelicdreamz.com
JIE-Doll		X		http://www.angelicdreamz.com
Jpopdolls		X	X	http://www.jpopdolls.net/store/home.php?cat=11
KazeKidz		X	X	http://www.kazekidz.com/

Company	Realistic	Exaggerated	Fantasy	Website
Kim Lasher BJDs		X	X	http://www.lasherbjds.com/
KizDolls	X		X	http://www.kizdolls.com/
La Legende de Temps	X	X	X	http://lltdoll.weebly.com/
Latidoll		X	X	http://www.latidoll.com/
Leeke World	X	X	X	http://www.leekeworld.com/En/
LINA ChouChou		X		http://linachouchou.com/
Little Monica	X	X		http://www.littlemonica.co.kr/
LoongSoul		X	X	http://www.loongsouldoll.com/
Lume Doll	X	X		http://www.lumedoll.com/
Luts		X	X	http://www.eluts.com/
Marti Presents	X			http://marti.presents.pl/
Mecha Angel	X			http://dollsoom.com/eng/mechaangel.html
Musedoll		X		http://musedoll.com/
Napi Doll			X	http://www.napidoll.com/
nDoll	X	X	X	http://ndoll.net/skin/shop.php
Nine9 Style		X		http://www.nine9style.com/
Nobility Doll	X	X		http://www.nobilitydoll.com/
Notdoll Lab		X	X	http://www.notdolllab.com/
Ocean Moon		X		http://oceanmoon.net/
Olleaf		X		http://www.olleaf.com/
Or-Doll	X		X	http://or-doll.com/
Peak's Woods		X	X	http://www.peakswoods.com
Pipos		X	X	http://piposland.com/
PixyDoll		X		http://www.pixydoll.com/
PlanetDoll	X		X	http://www.pixydoll.com/
Pluto Dolls	X			http://hadess.org/dolls/index.htm
POPO Doll		X	X	http://www.popodoll.com/
R.A.On Dream	X			http://www.raon-dream.com/shop/main/intro.php
Raurencio Studio	X	X	X	http://www.raurencio.com/
ResinSoul	X		X	http://www.resinsoul.com/
Ringdoll		X	X	http://www.ringdoll.com/index.html
RosenLied		X		http://www.rosenlied.com/eng/index.php
Rosette School of Dolls		X		http://www.dollsoom.com/
Secretdoll		X		http://www.secretdoll.com/
SinyLand	X		X	http://sinyland.com/en/
Slinky Neko		X		http://slinkyneko.com/
Soom Emporium	X	X	X	http://dollsoom.com/soom/
Soul Doll	X		X	http://www.souldoll.com/
Spirit Doll		X		http://www.spiritdoll.net/

Company	Realistic	Exaggerated	Fantasy	Website
Sseiren Doll	X			http://sseiren.com/
Ssin (Joadoll)		X		http://www.i-joadoll.com/
Sugarble		X	X	http://sugarble.com/
SupiaDoll		X		http://supiadollz.net/index.php
SWITCH (formerly Sonyeongi)		X		http://from-switch.com/
The Gem (Soom)	X	X	X	http://dollsoom.com/eng/gem.html
The Old World	X	X	X	http://www.towdoll.com/OldWorld/
The Sleeping Elf		X	X	http://littlebloomers.tripod.com/thesleepingelf/
Volks USA	X	X		http://www.volksusa.com/index.html
Weepy Doll		X		http://weepydoll.com/
WithDoll		X	X	http://www.withdoll.com/
Yuusui's Doll Workshop	X	X		http://yuusuisdollworkshop.wordpress.com/

Don't think for a minute that this list is complete or everyone will agree with me. It's merely a starting point.

Body types

While you're perusing those dolls' promo photos, keep your desired body types in mind as well. You can choose from several different types:

Female body types

- Model body - tall and curvy with long legs, usually with a small, realistic head

- Fashion model body - tall and with huge breasts, reminiscent of a fashion doll (like Barbie or Tonner)

- Mature female body - tall and medium curves, head size can vary

- Small bust female body - less mature female body

- Youthful female body - straight (or flat-chested and larger-hipped) female body

- Slim female body - slim and willowy female body

- Girl body - short, girlish body

Male body types

- Super hero body - tall and muscular, usually includes a smaller head

- Regular male body - tall and mature, more realistically proportioned than a super hero body

- Boy body - slim, narrow and willowy figure

Unisex body types

Most unisex bodies are tiny unsexed resin bodies (usually 27cm or less), and you can define your character based on the face-up, wig, and outfit.

Other body types

Other types of bodies also exist: from cutie pear-shaped girls (check out Dust of Dolls' Püns) to mermaids, centaurs, robotic bodies, and multiple-limb fantasy types. Pretty much anything you can imagine is available!

Staying organized - Flickr galleries and wish lists

Excitement in purchasing your first BJD can be overwhelming. Your wish list of dolls is going to grow over time, so use these two handy tips for staying organized and preventing impulse purchases. You'll want to keep at least one wish list gallery on Flickr, and one BJD spreadsheet, including cost and priority.

Flickr Gallery

Set up a free photo account on Flickr. This is a great way to view actual owner photos of BJDs, not just promotional photos.

It still isn't as good as experiencing the dolls in person--their feel and articulation-- but it is a great way to see a face!

1. Visit www.flickr.com and click on **Sign Up**.

2. Follow the instructions on Flickr for signing up for a free Flickr photo account. You can connect this account to your Yahoo! ID if you like.

3. Browse around on Flickr for BJDs in the style, size or aesthetic you like. When you see a doll you like, add it to your **Favorites**, by pressing the little star icon next to the Favorites button.

4. Once you have some favorites, you can view them in your account by clicking on the **You** tab, and then going to **Favorites**.

5. Find the BJDs you like best from these photos--you may notice a recurring sculpt--and then click on its thumbnail.

6. Next, under the **Actions** tab, click on **Add to Gallery**.

7. Choose **Create a New Gallery**, and name it BJD Wish List, or something that you'll find easy to remember.

8. Then, click on the gallery's name to add the photo to your gallery.

Galleries can hold up to 18 photos, and you can add descriptions of the items and notes. It's a great and gorgeous way to keep your wish list organized, and you can celebrate the beauty of other artists' wonderful photos, while giving them a compliment at the same time. You can add notes to the photos--such as the resin color you prefer or the company's website--next to the photos as well.

Post a link to your gallery on BJDs for Beginners (www.bjdsforbeginners.com) if you'd like to share!

Now, move on to the next step.

Pricing Spreadsheet

In addition to your photo gallery, which will function like a shopping window, you'll also want to create a wish list spreadsheet on your computer. I know, it sounds a little dorky, but BJDs are expensive. The last thing you want to do is to go into debt because of a hobby.

First, don't forget that BJDs *are* a hobby. As much fun as they are, remember to stick to your assigned budget. Whether you transfer money from your main checking account to Paypal on a monthly basis or work with cash, it's important to keep track of your hobby money and never go over budget. Borrowing from next month's allotment or from a projected sale is a slippery slope and can lead to bad habits.

When you stick to your budget, you'll find your collection more rewarding, and you'll treasure your dolls much more. You will plan more carefully, anticipate their arrival with more excitement, and you'll enjoy them more. It's embarrassing to have to talk to your spouse or significant other (or your parents!) about how much money you need for your doll hobby if you accidentally overspend. So don't do it! Not ever.

You won't have to if you budget well. Many companies and dealers offer lay-away, and I recommend those options and/or cash and debit payments instead of credit. It's a more fulfilling way to indulge in any hobby.

Do a budget. Planning how to spend your money is a must for every high-end collector.

On to your budget spreadsheet, which should include the following information:

Sculpt	Company	Price	Details	Size	Eyes	Wigs	Priority
Vampire Hucky	Peak's Woods	$312	white skin, girl make-up	FOF, 26 cm	14 mm	6/7	1
Lady Bee	Peak's Woods	$375	White skin, face-up	FOB, 58 cm	14 mm	7/8	2
?? tan LE	Peak's Woods	$644	face-up, tan skin summer LE	FOC, 58 cm	18 mm	8/9	1

Fill in all the dolls from your wish list gallery on this spread sheet, then sort the dolls by priority. Now you have a visual list of the dolls you'd like to add your collection.

Visit each company's website, and see if they have lay-away available. Most companies require that you spend a certain amount or split your payment into two or three payments, so plan to save first. You might also check Den of Angels or other online forums, or search for "[your doll company] event" in Google, and see if your company has a history of doing any sales or specials. Many companies have promotions around Christmas or the New Year. This will help you budget and plan.

You can also look if these dolls come up for sale previously loved (on the secondary market). In this book, I will show you easy ways to restore a BJD--you can restring a doll, sand and de-yellow a doll, and remove minor staining--but there are a few things that probably can't be fixed (like Sharpie marker and heavy smoke odor).

Then, start saving. Don't forget-- whenever you see a new doll you love, add it to your list first. Remember to consider: do you like this doll as much as the others in your gallery and spreadsheet? Does she fit with your general aesthetic? If so, add her to your list. Consider all these things before you buy, and you'll save yourself a lot of time and hassle.

Pricing and quality

Why are some BJDs more costly than others? Size actually doesn't make much of a difference in production cost, as it costs as much to make a large doll as it does to make a small one.

Production location

Dolls made in China cost less than dolls manufactured in Japan and Korea. I haven't yet found a significant quality difference, except in some of the details of the hands and feet. Mostly it's stylistic and sculpting differences.

Materials

There are several types of resin. French resin has a smooth, shiny finish and is available in different colors. It is considered to be less toxic than the opaque polyurethane resin, but you may need to buff it with Magic Eraser to get a matte, skin-like texture. Also, it is more expensive than original resin, since it's often mixed with a UV protector as well. It's more difficult to pour. In the past, French resin seemed to yellow more quickly, but this problem seems to have been fixed.

Keep in mind that tan or darker colored dolls are also usually more expensive. Colors and dyes are added to the resin and must be matched and poured correctly. Some colored dolls may fade unevenly. Sanding isn't recommended, either, as the color may become uneven or splotchy.

Jointing and articulation

Usually, the more articulated the doll, the more expensive. Look for flanged (or covered) joints. This makes the joints less mechanical-looking and hides the elastic string. Double-jointed elbows and knees can be a plus: these allow the doll to kneel sitting on her heels, for example, or touch her face with her hand.

My personal belief is to sacrifice some articulation in the name of beauty. That is, the more articulation your doll has, the less attractive the joints are.

I love Peak's Woods' jointing. The Fairy of Color body sculpt has perfect knees and elbows--and the torso is unbelievably gorgeous. Sure, you can find more articulated dolls, but I don't think you can find a more curvy, beautiful body than a Peak's Woods Fairy of Color. They have a great balance of posing ability, articulation, and joint attractiveness.

Sculpting details

Usually more expensive sculpts will have detailing in their hands, fingers, soles of their feet, and faces. All in all, when comparison shopping, just be certain you're getting the doll *you* like the most.

Pay special attention to these details while shopping:

- Hands: find a photo of the actual doll touching her face, or her hand close to her face. Make sure her hand is proportional. Another bonus: often, alternate posed hands are available.

- Feet: I love a molded foot. Dolls should be able to stand on their bare feet while still having molded arches. Make sure you examine the toes and that you like them.

- Ears: Many times, a doll's ears are covered by their wigs. I can't tell you how many dolls I have sold because I haven't liked their ears! Ears are hard to sculpt.

- Nose: You may find you collect dolls with a particular type of nose sculpt--buttons, upturned, straight, tiny, realistic. It's very strange: I have a heart for upturned noses.

- Jawlines and chins: If you can find profile shots of your doll's face at different angles, this is very helpful. Often, you can't tell what a doll really looks like until you see it from different angles. Female dolls with masculine jawlines just don't do it for me anymore.

- Eye sculpt: Not just the size of the eye socket, but check how close together they are, and how deep the sockets are also. That will make a difference in how easy the eyes are to put in and aim. If the manufacturer's photo doesn't look quite right, yours probably won't either.

- Body shape: Do you want a waif? Do you want a model body? A normal girl? Make sure you like how she poses and sits before you order.

Matching resin from another company's body is another option, if you fall in love with a pricey face. Do some research before investing in a full doll. You'll need to be sure the neck circumference is about the same for both bodies as well.

Basic doll, full set, or limited edition

A full set BJD includes a face-up, wig, outfit and shoes, and sometimes has had the seam lines sanded down. Basic dolls are usually sold a la carte, and you add the services you want to your doll.

Limited edition dolls are limited either in number or to their ordering period. They may be a limited face or body sculpt, resin color, or include a limited face-up. This means the make-up style is created for this doll only--not that the make up is a more natural style (with less face paint). These dolls cost more, and they are usually valued more highly on the secondary market, as well.

Finishing touches

Does your doll include applied eyelashes, or do you have to add them? How detailed is her face-up? What sort of eyes does she have--glass or acrylic? What quality is her wig? Do you choose the colors or are they "random"? Does she come sanded? All of these things increase the doll's quality, and also her price.

Resin seams

If your doll doesn't specifically say sanding is included, chances are you will need to sand some seam lines when he or she arrives. This isn't difficult, but is a little time-consuming.

Getting what you pay for

Finally, as in all things in life, you get what you pay for when it comes to a ball-jointed dolls. Keep in mind that if you spend $100 on a BJD, you will get a $100 BJD. If you spend $500, your doll will be a higher quality.

My advice is to get the one doll you *really love*, not several dolls you mostly like. In the end, most collectors end up going this way. You might as well save yourself the hassle of selling unwanted dolls and start saving for the one you really want. Take advantage of lay-away if necessary. Many manufacturers and doll shops offer this option.

Themes and customization

The best part about ball-jointed dolls is that once you've ordered one, that's not the only thing you can do. You can customize your doll just the way you want: whether you want to make a specific character, or a specific look for your doll who can be many characters, you can do just what you like and make your doll uniquely your own.

You can choose the outfits, and change your doll on a monthly basis, or as often as you like. Holiday outfits are available, and custom doll seamstresses are everywhere on Den of Angels and Etsy, just waiting to take your order.

No one else needs to have a doll exactly like yours.

Face-ups

Did you know that your doll's face-up is painted by hand? Many manufacturers, including Peak's Woods, will paint a face-up according to your request. You might also order a blank doll and have a local artist paint the face for you.

Peak's Woods charges $10-$20 over the regular price if you order a custom face-up. You can be as specific as you like, such as: "I'd like my doll painted like your limited edition white skin Sky doll from 'The Glamour' collection." Or, "I'd like Cue painted in purples, whatever the artist feels like doing."

Your doll's face-up will wear over time, so you will have a chance of getting a new and different face-up for your doll. You can even own more than one sculpt of a doll and see what a difference a face-up makes!

Eye types and measurements

Usually, when you order a doll, you'll be able to see on the website what is included. You may want to consider additional eyes. If the millimeter measurement isn't listed online, measure your doll's eye socket from the outside corner to the inside corner.

Glass eyes are beautiful and haunting, but tend to be more expensive than acrylic. The most beautiful eyes on the market are soft glass (silicone), but these are the most expensive of all.

Wig types and measurements

Your doll's wig size should also be listed in the description from the manufacturer. The measure is actually an inch measurement.

If you need to measure yourself, take a tailor's tape measure (a flexible one), and wrap it around your doll's forehead, just above the ears, and around the nape of the neck, where you'd want the wig to fit, about where the head cap is, or just a little bit lower. If the inch measurement, such as 8-3/4", falls between eight and nine inches, it's a size 8/9 wig.

Notes about yellowing

Now would be a good time for a few words on handling your doll and on the delicacy of resin.

Regardless of how resin is stored, it's not a stable material. Over time, even in a dark room with no light or handling, it will age and yellow, simply because of its chemical make-up. How you handle deal with this is up to you.

Storing your doll in a lower light environment will help slow the process. Keeping her safe from pets and oil, unnecessary UV rays and UV light will help, too. But does that mean you have to wear gloves every time you handle her? You can, if you choose. If you do, your doll will probably yellow less over time, depending on *the quality of the resin*.

However, if the resin wasn't mixed properly, or if it isn't a high quality resin, it's quite possible all the precautions you take won't help slow the normal yellowing process. Maybe we BJD collectors should take a collective breather and relax a moment.

Sure, it doesn't hurt to wash your hands and keep oil away from your doll, but I don't think it's necessary to store your doll in a box. I keep my beauties behind glass, but that's for kitty protection. (Cats adore mohair wigs, let me warn you now.) I don't expose my dolls to direct sunlight on a daily basis, either.

But consider that a gently yellowed doll, with *even* yellowing, can be quite gorgeous in her own right. My first large ABJD is Peak's Woods Sky. She is white skin, and she has seen a lot in her life so far. She is not as white as her newer sisters anymore, but I find her equally beautiful.

I also purchased a gorgeous normal skin Mintie on the secondary market, who has evenly yellowed to the perfect skin tone. It more than likely depends on the resin quality, I'm sure, than anything you do to a doll. But don't panic if your doll yellows a little.

Purchasing your BJD

If you're new to ball-jointed dolls, you wouldn't think I'd need to dedicate an entire chapter on how to purchase a BJD. However, if this is your first time buying a ball-jointed doll, it may be a little harder than it looks.

You already have a list of doll companies you like, and you should have a gallery and a prioritized wish list by now. The time has come to make your first purchase. Here are some things to consider before you buy.

To consider before your purchase

First, determine your budget. Setting yourself a monthly or bi-weekly doll allowance is the best way to keep your hobby (or any other expenditure) under control. Limiting yourself is also a good way to keep your spending in check, to prevent credit card debt and arguing over money with a significant other.

Just because you have a meager doll allowance does *not* mean you can't afford the ball-jointed doll of your dreams. You'll just need a little longer to pay for it. There are several things you can do to get there faster:

First, consider lay-away. Many dealers offer this option, and it's an excellent way to afford the doll you want--especially if you're considering a limited edition. Many doll manufacturers also offer lay-away on their websites, but you may need to ask.

Second, start saving now. If you can save up a chunk of cash, you can have either a larger portion for the down payment of a lay-away, or you may be able to pay for your entire doll up front. You can also add to your doll budget in smaller ways: cut down on the number of trips you take to the coffee shop, combine trips to the grocery store to save on gas, plan your meals and eat at home, take your meals to work instead of eating out for lunch, and so on.

If you're still living at home, you may be in a tighter situation. It helps if a family member gets into the hobby with you, but if you can't, let it be known that you'd like to start saving for *this* BJD. Be sure of the doll you want first and call him or her by name. Offer to do extra chores around the house (or other people's homes) for pay. Get a job, if you can, even if it isn't what you want to do for the rest of your life. See if you have anything valuable you might be able to sell on eBay or a garage sale. Babysit, especially for other BJD collectors who are trying to write books and keep from going absolutely insane.

Third, consider upgrading your collection. I know, I know--I get a lot of flack for even suggesting this. If you already collect other dolls, take an inventory. Be sure you include the doll's name, maker and current value. If you don't know the value of the doll, look it up on eBay. Now--look at that list carefully. In fact, I recommend creating a list in spreadsheet format, so you can add up the total value of your dolls. (I like to keep what I originally paid for the doll on that list, too.) Is it a large number? How much do you *love* each of those dolls?

Notice I'm not asking how much you *like* the dolls on that list. How much do you *love* them? Which would you rather have: those dolls, sitting in boxes in your garage (I've been there, too!), or a brand new BJD who can be many, many characters, simply by changing a wig? You could get much closer to your choice of BJD by selling a few of those "liked" dolls.

If you aren't comfortable selling on eBay yourself, you can try the DollPage Show & Sell, or a consignment eBay shop. The best one I have found so far is Kathie's Fashion Dolls. She charges a reasonable commission for items that sell for less than $200 (and even lower commission for items selling for $200 or more). She lists the item, completes the sale, packs everything up for you, completes all the feedback, worries about the happy customer for you, and writes you a check. Last time I sold on eBay myself, I ended up paying close to her percentage after my eBay and Paypal fees alone. Her eBay ID is **barbiekenscout**.

After working out your budget, consider the doll's production time. Usually, 30-45 days is a typical quote, however, it can take much longer. After it's placed, your order cannot be cancelled or changed. The resin will be cast when the weather is right. Why it takes so long is somewhat of a mystery, but it has to do with the number of people in the company, the hand-made nature of the dolls, and the cultural differences.

Be prepared to wait if you order a doll that isn't in stock. You may want to check the company's feedback on Den of Angels before you place your order, just to be sure they are reputable and aren't backlogged.

Finally, you should consider what you would settle for: Does your doll have to be brand new, or would you consider a used doll? There are lots of places to find used dolls, but they do come with risks:

- Smoke smell or other odors - Resin is fairly porous, so it's difficult to get out odors.

- Stringing problems - When you buy a used doll, the doll may need restringing. But I will show you how later in the techniques section.

- Normal wear and tear - BJDs scratch, dent and wear over time. Is this acceptable to you? These can be sanded out, but you should consider this when buying a doll on the secondary market.

- Sculpt and resin tone combo - You may not be able to find the resin color (tan, for instance) and the sculpt you want. Sometimes, however, the secondary market is the only place to find limited edition dolls.

- Uneven yellowing - Used dolls, depending on their environment, may have some yellowing, just because that's what resin does. If the doll is white or normal resin, this can usually be fixed somewhat with sanding. Colored resin doesn't lend itself well to sanding, so keep this in mind.

- Broken dolls - Are all the fingers, toes and joints intact? You can purchase replacement parts from the manufacturer, but sometimes the yellowed body won't match the replacement piece.

- Bargain prices versus retail prices - Often, sellers expect to get what they paid (and sometimes more) out of a doll they have listed.

- Clear photos - How clear are the photos of the doll? You wouldn't want a surprise face-up on a $400 doll.

You can fix or avoid many of these problems with one simple technique: research! Take the time to:

- Look up the seller's feedback. Use multiple sources, and don't be afraid to ask for references.

- Ask for additional photos. Don't be shy. Most sellers want you to buy their doll and are happy to oblige.

- Ask detailed questions about the doll. "Does she have all her fingers and toes? Does she stand on her own? Does she have an even skin tone? Any yellowing? Any staining? Any dents, dings or breakage? Has she been around smoke or pets?"

If you stick to these tips and make sure not to rush into any "great deals" or things that sound too good to be true, you should have great success on the secondary market. Most deals that sound too good to be true, are.

Do remember: odors, yellowed colored resin, and permanent marker stains: these can't be fixed easily.

In person

The best way you can buy a doll is in person. You can find BJDs at doll shows and conventions, at BJD meet-ups, and in a few doll shops. I live in southern California, and I have to drive to Los Angeles for the closest BJD store in my area. However, there are at least three or four doll clubs that meet around here regularly. That's a great way to see BJDs in person.

Seeing a variety of BJDs in real life (instead of just in photos) is the best way to discover what aesthetics you prefer and what styling you like best. You'll be able to ask the owners questions about how the doll poses, how easy it is to find clothing, wigs, shoes, and more. You'll get a chance to see hybrid dolls (dolls with one manufacturer's head on another manufacturer's body), as well as creative and unique face-ups.

Additionally, when you see dolls in person, you can get a feel for your ideal scale. Hearing the abbreviations SD, MSD and YoSD and calculating 58 cm, 42 cm and 27 cm into inches (about 22 3/4", 16 1/2" and a little over 10 1/2") are one thing, but seeing a 58 cm BJD in full regalia is something completely different.

Even if you attend a meet in which no BJDs are for sale, you can still get a better idea of what you like. But a real doll store? With in-stock BJDs? Danger, danger! You'd better have saved money in your pocket before you go!

Do consider lay-away. It's a good friend and much better than credit when it comes to budgeting for BJDs.

Online

Of course, if you can't find a meet in your area, or if no one is selling the doll you want, buying your doll online is another option.

The nice thing about ordering a doll online is that you will be getting your very own custom BJD, made just for you. You customize the make-up, color of eyes and wig from many BJD companies.

Personally, I prefer going through a doll dealer when it's available. The reason: you can often save on international shipping prices, and I feel good supporting my favorite doll shop, too. Often, the dealer may have the BJD I want in stock, so I don't have to wait as long, either.

My favorite BJD manufacturer, Peak's Woods, does not sell through US dealers anymore. They sell only from their website. You'll need to visit their website to place your order. It's easy--most manufacturers have user-friendly English language. Many sites also have frequent shopper points you can use toward future purchases.

Keep in mind some companies will call their large, mini and tiny dolls by different names. Large are sometimes called 1/3 scale dolls, minis are 1/4 scale dolls, and tinies are 1/6 scale. Peak's Woods has renamed them Fairies of Color, Fairies of Bugs and Fairies of Fairies of Fairytales.

50

Before placing an order with any doll manufacturer, you'll want to check their feedback. Some doll companies have a very slow turnaround, and you'll want to be aware of this before placing your order. The message forum Den of Angels has an entire section of company feedback for BJD companies and dealers. If you can't find the company, do a forum-wide search on the company name. You want to be sure the manufacturer has a good reputation, and delivery times around 45 days or so, which is typical of the industry.

When you place your order, you may have the option to choose the body type, skin color, and whether you want a face-up. A good face-up will cost around $50-75. Artist commissions can cost much more than this, so if you like the company face-up, it's worth the price.

I used to believe that you should buy the specific shoes that were sold on the BJD website as well. Now, I'm not convinced that's important anymore. Check the measurements. If the girl's feet are under 8 cm, and the boys are under 9 cm, they won't be hard to fit. Those are standard sizes for large dolls.

Using Paypal is probably the safest method of payment for your doll. A credit card would also be fine, but I wouldn't recommend paying with a debit card online. You should be aware that some credit cards will charge you an overseas processing fee for using the card at a Korean, Japanese or Chinese company. Also, you'll want to be sure that the website starts with https:// at the top before you enter in any credit card information.

Keep in mind that when you use Paypal or your credit card, you are offered some protection with overseas purchases. Check to make sure your card doesn't charge any processing fees for cross-the-border transactions before using it. If the shipping time is much longer than 45 days, your buyer protection plan is pretty much annulled through Paypal, which is why it pays to check company feedback.

On the secondary market

Shopping the secondary market, such as message boards, eBay or the DollPage Show & Sell, is another great option. You can find reasonable prices and good deals, if you are willing to learn some basic maintenance techniques.

- I cannot stress this enough: be sure to do your research.

- Don't forget to compare the manufacturer's new price to the used doll's price. Not having to wait should *not* increase the price of a doll. (Don't be an impatient collector!)

- Don't forget to check out the feedback of the seller.

- Include shipping costs in the calculation of the price.

- Make sure you have seen clear photos of the doll.

- Ask about the doll's condition. Can she stand on her own? Does she need restringing? Is she yellowed or stained? Even or darker spots? Any chips, cracks or dings? Any missing, cracked or re-glued fingers or toes?

- Do *not* mark your payment as a gift. You'll lose buyer protection from Paypal if you do this. Opt to calculate fees and cover them, if the seller insists.

- Do you like the face-up, or will you change it? Include that in the price and negotiate, if you can.

- Instead of paying extra for faster shipping, use the money for insurance instead.

- Does your seller have a return policy, in case you don't like the doll?

- Again, smoke is really hard to get out of resin. Keep this in mind when you're shopping for a used doll. Ask if the doll is from a non-smoking environment, and if it's from the original owner.

Keep in mind that it's expensive to ship a heavy resin doll safely, and the US Postal service charges more for shipping oversized boxes. Sometimes it's less to ship UPS ground, or have the seller unstring the doll's legs from the body (keeping the loop tied) and include the elastic. The doll torso and legs can be shipped safely wrapped in bubble wrap, and it's usually easy to restring. Be sure to let your seller know when the doll has arrived, and leave positive feedback.

I've found lots of bargain dolls on the secondary market. It's important to know what you're getting and understand that there may be differences between what you consider to be a BJD in good condition and what others consider good condition. In the next chapter, I'll teach you to maintain your doll as well as bring your bargain finds into beautiful condition.

Caring for your BJD

Every ball-jointed doll owner needs to know the basics about caring for his or her new ball-jointed friend. It's easy, and you'll love getting to know your new boy or girl. Let's start with the basic supplies you'll need to have on hand.

55

BJD supplies

Before your doll arrives, you can stock up on the following must-have supplies (yes, the store brand works as well):

- Magic Eraser
- Mr. Superclear
- Hemostats (available at stores with medical supplies or fishing equipment)
- Pliers
- Pipe cleaners and/or restringing tool
- Extra elastic cord
- Mack's silicone ear plugs
- Dr. Scholl's Moleskin Plus
- Super glue
- Jewelry-grade sand paper (220, 400 and 600 grit)
- Face mask
- Rubbing alcohol or 100% acetone

Additionally, you might consider:

- Chalk pastels (*not* oil)
- Large high-quality round brush
- Small angled brush
- #1 round brush (I like Mr. Brush)
- Superfine black water-soluble marker
- Liquitex gloss medium
- Watercolor pencils
- Aleene's Fast Grab Tacky glue (purple label)
- False eyelashes (human size, for large and mini BJDs)

The supply wars

There have been debates on which are the best and most efficient products to use on your resin dolls since BJDs were first introduced on the market. Here's my take on the subject; you can take it or leave it, since you will doubtless find contradictory evidence elsewhere.

> **Do** experiment with different products when customizing your doll. Find the products that work best for **you**.

Testors Dullcote or Mr. Superclear?

First, what is it? It's a resin spray, which acts as a sealant when you're doing a face-up (make-up) or body blush on your doll. You need it to first get pastels to adhere to your sanded doll, and a second coat to seal. Either Mr. Superclear or Testors Dullcote will do the trick. Both are safe for use with resin. (Please note that at the time of publication of this book, Krylon does *not* have any safe-for-resin sprays on the market.)

Why do I insist on Mr. Superclear instead of Testors? Well, I don't insist. I *prefer* UV cut matte spray MSC to Testors for several reasons. First, MSC offers UV protection that Testors doesn't. This may slow down the yellowing process. Second, though MSC is more difficult to find and a bit more expensive (though per size/weight, it comes out about equal), it flags (drips and runs) less; at least out here in dry, sunny San Diego. I know you'll hear this again and again, but if you just spent $300 on a doll, why complain about spending $11 on a can of sealant that will help keep her pretty longer? It's hardly a difference, comparatively.

Third, I find it works a lot better on my resin dolls than Testors. Testors attracts more dirt than MSC, in my opinion. I'm messy and clumsy when working with chalk, and I get color everywhere. I can remove mistakes easily from MSC, but I can't as easily with Testors.

Finally, I can never find Testors in my area. Dullcote is always out of stock! It's annoying. For small dolls or face-ups, however, I'm sure Testors works just as well. I've used it a couple of times, and other artists swear by it. Perhaps I'm using too much or am simply too clumsy.

I order Mr. Superclear from Junkyspot (www.junkyspot.com). It's important to get relatively fresh cans--that is, cans that haven't been sitting around for years--or they won't spray evenly. Since Junkyspot runs out from time to time and rotates stock, I know they are fresh. I also buy mine in packs of three, in case a friend needs one.

Using acetone on resin

Did I recommend you purchase acetone for a resin doll? I did, in fact. Here's the truth about acetone.

Yes, applying acetone to your doll's face-up will remove it. Just take care when using it. Always apply small amounts on a clean cotton ball or Q-tip, and never put a dirty cotton ball on the doll's face.

Yes, applying acetone to resin temporarily softens the surface of resin. Sanding or even using a toothpick on resin softened with acetone will scratch and dent your doll. Ask me how I know! Use a tiny brush instead.

No, you do *not* need to rinse acetone off with water or soap. Acetone will evaporate when dry, and you *must* let it dry. If you wash your doll with soap and water while the resin is still soft, you risk denting or scratching. If you wish to wash your doll with soap and water *after* the acetone has evaporated, who am I to argue?

Yes, you need to use acetone in a well-ventilated area. Be sure to protect your eyes. Use it sparingly. Never soak your doll or pieces of your doll in acetone.

If you are reluctant to use acetone, try Magic Eraser, used dry. For more power, you can use the sponge damp, but keep in mind this will remove face-ups and body blushing also.

The next best thing is rubbing alcohol, but sometimes alcohol isn't enough to remove a face-up, if that's your goal.

Another commonly used cleaner is Winsor & Newton's Brush Cleaner. Loads of people on Den of Angels have been using this product for removing face-ups and cleaning dolls, including my editor Melissa. Interestingly, the active ingredient in this product is ethanol.

More notes on supplies

You can use your 40% or 50% off coupons from Michaels, Jo-Ann Fabrics or other craft stores in your neighborhood to invest in artist-quality pencils and pastels. If you're using them on a precious BJD, why wouldn't you spend a little more and get the best quality you can?

Once your doll arrives, you can determine which additional eyes and wigs she needs according to her face-up coloring (technically, you could buy these in advance, but you'll run the risk of purchasing wigs and eyes that don't match). I like to have a nice selection on hand--make sure to get a range of colors and styles, including both dark and light shades.

Measuring eyes isn't intuitive. The sizes are listed in millimeters. The size refers to the entire width of the eye socket, or the entire diameter of the eye. Measure either the doll's existing eye diameter, or her eye socket from the inside corner to the outside. Make sure you use a ruler with a millimeter measurement on it. Large BJDs can vary a lot--Peak's Woods dolls wear between 16mm and 20mm, depending on the sculpt. More realistic sculpts can wear 12mm. Some tiny dolls wear only 3mm.

A note about eyes: soft glass (silicone) eyes are only available in odd sizes. In this case, size up one millimeter. Also, you'll note that the size of the iris may be shaped differently in some acrylic styles, and that the iris may be smaller or larger. Generally, a smaller iris with more white space can look more realistic, but can also make your doll look a bit "wild eyed" if they are too small for the sculpt.

Regarding wigs, you'll want several styles and colors for different looks. Often, a doll will have eyebrows painted a specific color, and this determines an "ideal" hair color for the doll. However, just because your doll has darkly painted brows doesn't mean you shouldn't use a blonde wig.

You can find out measurements from the manufacturer's website, or by measuring them yourself. A doll's wig measurement is the circumference around her head in inches. You'll need a flexible ruler or a piece of string, which you loop around the doll's bald head about where the wig cap would end: on the forehead and above the ears.

Your measurement might be 8-3/4" for a large doll. In this case, your doll would wear a size 8/9 wig. For mini dolls, many measure between seven and eight inches, which corresponds to size 7/8. Yo-sized dolls often wear a size 6/7, as their heads measure between six and seven inches.

***Don't** be afraid to experiment with wigs and try unusually colored hair or mohair wigs on your beautiful new BJD!*

Peak's Woods Fairies of Color technically measure over nine inches, so they wear a 9/10. However, if the wig cap is stretchy, such as in Monique or J-Pop wigs, I've found the 8/9 wigs often work just as well.

See page 39 for photos on exactly where to measure for eyes and wigs.

Regular maintenance

Don't freak out now. This is the fun part. You don't even have to be crafty or artistic to succeed in this section!

Your doll needs regular maintenance? Certainly, if you want to keep him or her in the best condition. I have a few suggestions.

Cleaning your doll

Yearly, more or less, depending on where you keep your doll, you might want to clean her with a damp washcloth or Magic Eraser (for normal or white skin *unblushed* dolls only). Until you're an expert on stringing, this is something you can do without taking your doll apart, as long as you don't immerse her in water.

Why can't you get your doll wet? Well, you can. It's just that you don't want the elastic to get wet then allow it to get moldy, which is why I don't recommend full immersion. Additionally, if you've sueded your doll with moleskin, you don't want to get the moleskin damp. It will be a sticky mess.

For non-blushed dolls, on their bodies only (not on a painted face or painted nails, since this will remove face-up or nail polish), use Magic Eraser dry if the damp washcloth isn't getting the doll clean enough. Using a light touch and small, circular movements should remove any excess dirt or smudges, including clothing stains. For stubborn stains, you can get the sponge damp.

You may gently clean your doll's sealed face-up with a damp cloth, but keep in mind: some dolls' eyelashes are adhered with water-soluble glue, and they might come off if dampened, so keep the cloth away from the eyes.

> **Don't** use anything on your doll's face unless you are positive the face-up is sealed.

How can you tell if your doll's face-up is sealed? Did you order her directly from the factory? Then it is. Did you buy her on the secondary market? Ask the previous owner. Is the owner not sure? You can test the cloth in an inconspicuous area, such as the hairline, and see if any blush is removed. If it comes off, your doll's face-up is not sealed.

In this case, if your doll's face is dirty, you're in a bit of a fix. To seal the face-up, you need to use a resin spray (MSC or Testors), but this will also seal in the dirt. If you attempt to remove the dirt, you will probably also remove the face paint. (Again, you might want to ask me how I know!) My advice is to remove as much of the dirt as you dare with a damp Q-tip, using a *clean* Q-tip every time you touch the doll's face.

Then, seal the doll's face with at least two light coats of MSC, letting it dry well in-between. Don't forget to spray outside--and you may want to read the blushing tutorial first. You'll need Liquitex Gloss (or some other clear gloss varnish) when the spray is dry to add gloss to the lips and inner rims of the eyes.

Changing wigs

Changing your doll's wig is the easiest way to change her look. A simple wig change can radically change her character.

Technique

For this technique, you'll need a new wig.

1. To replace your doll's wig, hold the doll between your legs. You'll need both hands.

2. Using your fingers, stretch the wig inside the wig's cap.

3. Place both of your fingers over your doll's head cap (keeping the wig's tag in the back of the doll's head) and secure it on your doll's head over her ears.

4. Push the wig into place, off the doll's ears and forehead and back further onto her head.

5. Gently pull any tucked-in strands out from under the wig cap. Style as desired.

Changing your doll's wig, both style and color, is the fastest way to update her look and give your doll a new feel.

Don't be afraid to experiment with non-traditional colors or styles, even if you aren't a "blue-haired person." You might be surprised how well your new doll takes to a non-traditional color.

Common wig problems and fixes

Does your wig pop off the doll's head after it's in place? That might mean your wig is a bit small for your doll. Does it keep slipping forward or backward once it's in place? This means your wig is a little big.

Wig caps are an easy solution for wig problems. This is an easy way to make one. This technique can be used for wigged fashion dolls, too.

I have to give PamSD of Dollovely a shout-out for introducing me to this technique. I'm a huge fan. I first saw this at the 2009 December BJD convention in San Diego.

1. Cut slim strips of the faux moleskin.

2. Trim them into lengths wide enough to go over your doll's head cap (only).

3. Remove your doll's head cap.

4. Remove the paper from the moleskin to reveal the sticky part. Place the strips on your doll's head cap, with some gaps, but evenly spaced, as shown in these photos.

This will give the wig a little bit of grip instead of the slippery smooth resin surface. It should keep your wig in place.

Some collectors make a wig cap with low temperature hot glue (a dot or spiral pattern on the head cap), which also works well. Personally, I burn myself anytime I even look at a hot glue gun, so I prefer the faux moleskin.

Velcro is another option, but then you run the risk of pulling the hair out of the wig when you're adjusting it on the doll's head or removing it.

Permanent solution for a too-big wig

If your wig is slipping because it's too big for your dolls, you can fix it with this clever technique from Jen Eugley of JennyGrey designs.

Supplies

- Too-big wig
- Threaded needle
- Scissors
- 2" length of 1/4" elastic (length may need to be adjusted, depending on how big the wig is. When stretched, the elastic should go around one quarter of your doll's head.)

Technique

1. Turn the wig inside out. Hand stitch the center of the elastic to the center back of the wig, inside the wig cap.

2. Stretch each end of the elastic about twice as long as its resting length, and hand stitch in place, also to the inside of the wig cap. This allows to elastic to cinch in the extra circumference of the wig when the elastic is resting.

3. Try the wig on your doll. If it is still loose, you'll need to unstitch the elastic ends, and stretch them farther towards the front of the wig. Otherwise, you're finished.

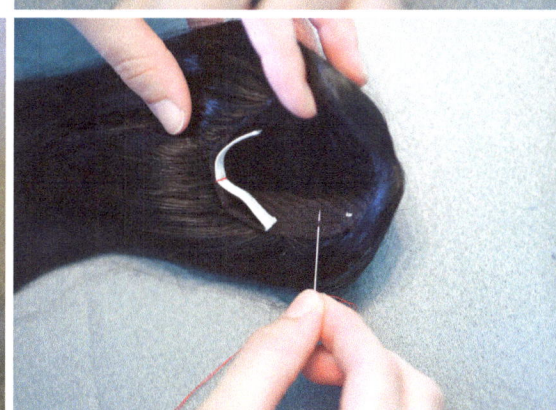

Replacing the head cap magnet

I'm about to show you how to replace your doll's eyes, which requires you to remove your doll's head cap. Sometimes, the magnets which hold the doll's head cap to the head fall out.

This is a common break among BJDs with head caps and face plates alike. Don't panic--all you need is a little super glue to fix the problem.

Supplies

- Super glue (I like Zap-a-Gap)

- Head cap

- Doll's head

Technique

Prepare all the parts before opening the glue. Make sure you work in a well-ventilated area.

Remove pliers, hemostats or other metal tools from your workspace for this technique. It's a pain if your magnet gets stuck to something else when you're trying to glue it in place.

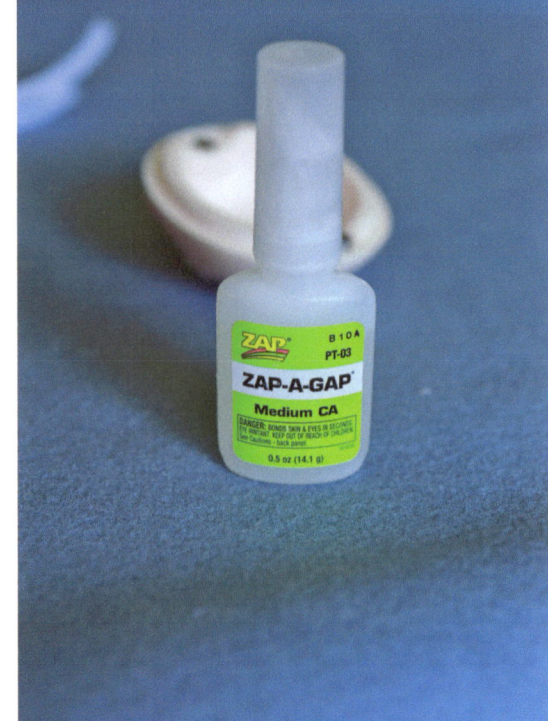

1. Place the magnet on the head cap to determine how it should fit in the head. Remember, magnets are polarized, and if you glue the magnet in upside down, you'll be in a bit of a mess. So take your time to get this part right. Set the head cap beside your work area, aligned in the proper direction with the magnet attached.

2. Next, apply just a drop or two of super glue in the head where the magnet is missing.

3. Using your fingers, drop the magnet in the hole in the proper orientation.

4. Press down lightly to ensure it's in the right place, and then firmly to adhere.

5. The glue bonds within 15-30 seconds, so you'll be able to replace your doll's head cap then. Make sure it's dry first!

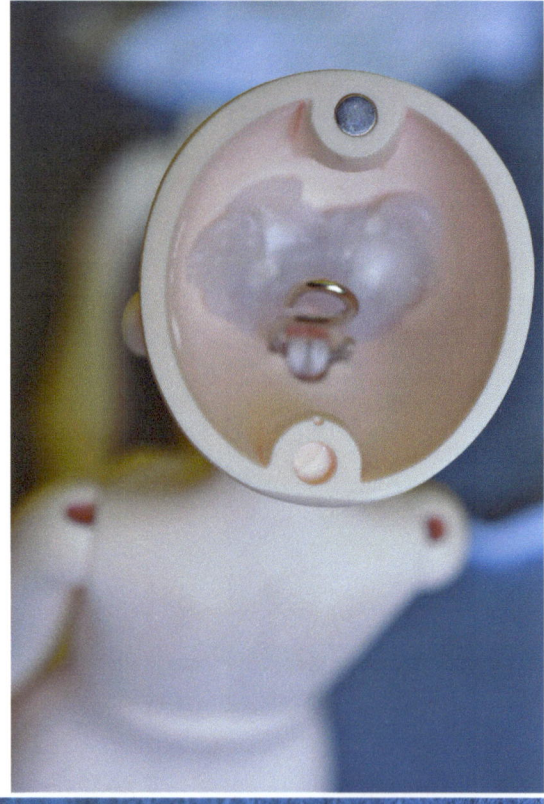

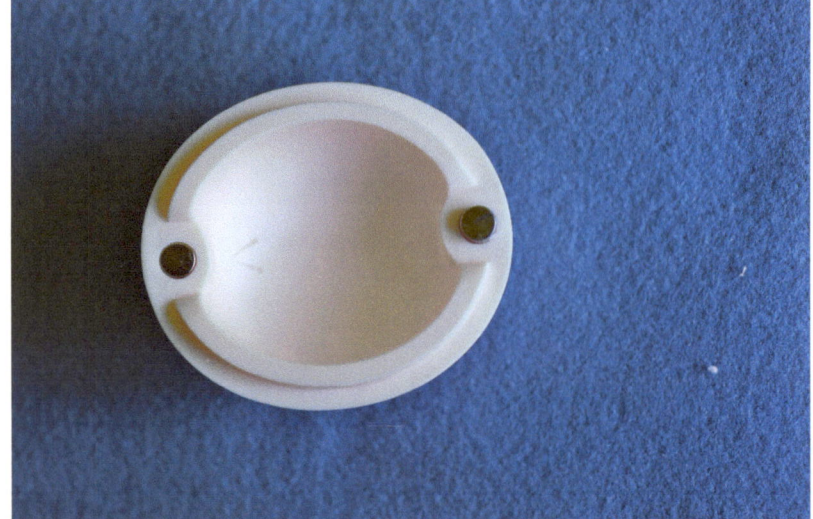

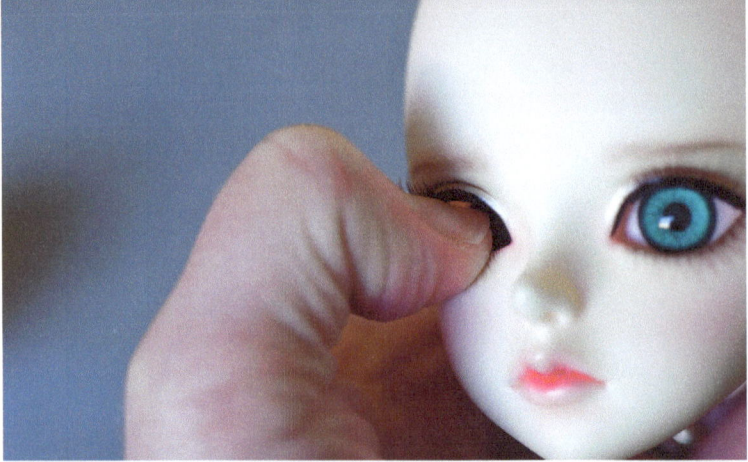

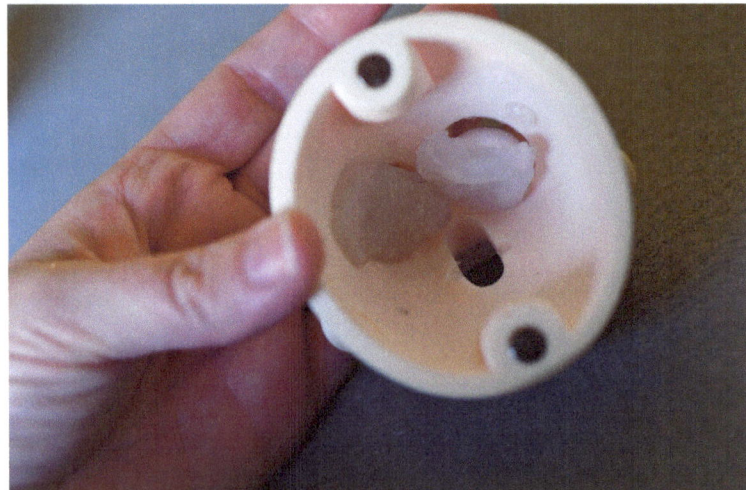
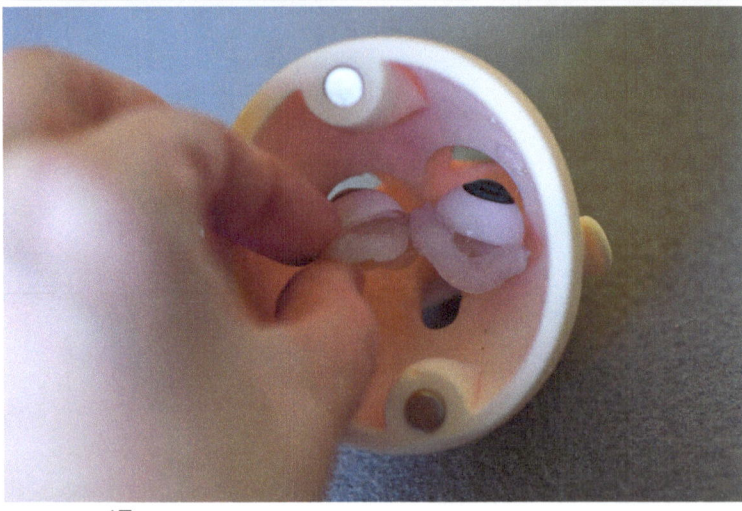

Changing eyes

If you don't change your doll's eyes, you're missing out! It isn't hard, and if you're careful with the eyelashes, you won't damage your doll. It's an easy, fun, and inexpensive way to change your doll's look.

Supplies

- Mack's silicone ear plugs or eye putty (use only putty for soft glass or silicone eyes, since Mack's will make these cloudy)
- pair of eyes

Technique

For the demonstration purposes, I removed my doll's head.

1. First, remove your doll's wig and head cap.
2. Peering inside the head, you'll see the existing eyes are held in with putty or silicone. Remove these first.
3. I start by pushing one of the eyeballs through the inside of the head (without touching the face or eyelashes), and then the other eye as well.
4. Once both eyes are poked inside, you can grab the putty and pull out both eyes at the same time.
5. If the putty hasn't dried completely, you may be able to reuse it. I prefer silicone, since it's clear, doesn't dry or crack, and it always comes out in one piece.
6. Be sure to remove all existing putty before inserting the new eyes. Soften the putty first in your hands until pliable.
7. Make a small sphere with the putty or silicone.
8. Push an eye down on one of the spheres, firmly enough to make it flat like a pancake. Now place inside the doll's head.

9. Aim the eye as desired, looking at the doll from the front, and use the excess putty from around the eye to hold it in place from the inside.

10. The tricky part is getting the second eye to line up to match the first one without making your doll look cross-eyed or wall-eyed. Be patient--this gets easier the more often you change your doll's eyes.

11. Hold the doll away from and close to you, to be sure you're happy with the effect before you replace her head cap and wig.

Good job! Now your doll has brand new eyes.

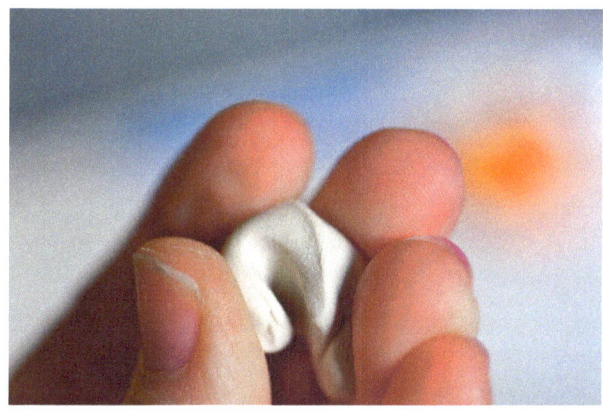

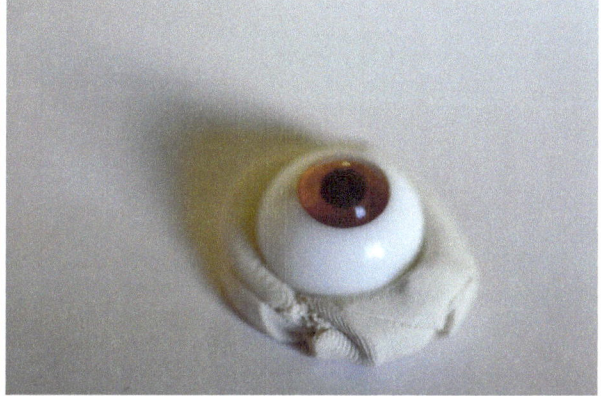

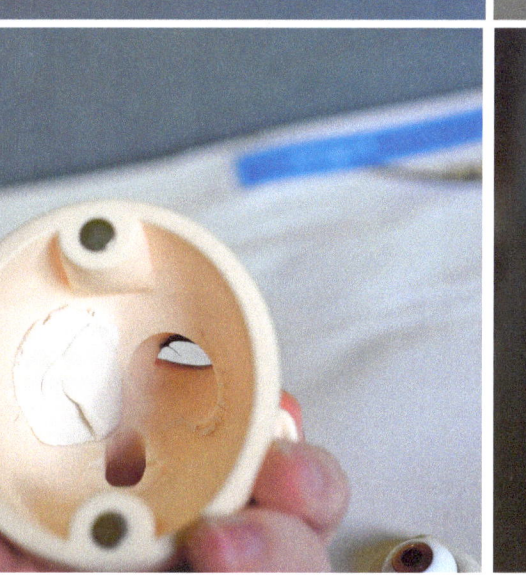

More on Eyes

Eye sizes

There's a lot to know about putting in eyes. While many sculpts are designed for a specific eye size, you can change the eye size up or down a few millimeters for different effects.

Model Viyol has 18 mm acrylic eyes on the right in Soho Green, and 20 mm acrylic eyes in hazel below.

Eye placement

If too much white shows above the iris, your doll will look afraid, like the photo of Viyol below. The trick to good eye placement is to align the pupils of the eyes, and match the white space equally on both sides of the eyes.

I find it's easiest to place eyes with more white showing at the bottom, so the doll is looking up, and slightly to the side.

Additional examples follow on the next pages.

Even with her eyes only slightly misaligned, Goldie looks off with these smaller diameter 14 mm glass eyes in violet.

On the left, her eyes are pointed too closely to her nose, making her look slightly cross-eyed.

On the right, her right eye isn't quite aligned with her left.

In the bottom photo, Goldie looks just about right. Notice how the left corners of the eyes have about the same amount of white showing.

On the next page, Goldie has had enough of these smaller diameter eyes, and would like to try a different color.

A high quality sculpt looks pretty sweet all the time--even when her eyes are in crooked.

Do be patient when experimenting with eyes. It takes a little practice to get them right, but it's oh-so-worth-it!

Larger eyes, such as the 16 mm acrylic in soho green (bottom left) and the 18 mm dark brown (right), are easier to align correctly, since they fit in the designed socket inside Goldie's head.

Smaller eyes with larger white area will generally give your BJD a more realistic look, while eyes with larger irises have a more anime aesthetic.

These are the three things to pay attention to when inserting eyes:

- the pupils are looking in the same direction

- no eye putty is showing around the eye

- you can't see around the eye into the head or eye mold (which would mean you need to use a larger eye size eye).

Basic customizing

This section includes some things you may want to do when you first receive your doll. It's a great way of getting to know her, as well as getting her to pose better and making her truly your own.

Sueding your doll so she will pose and stand alone

This is also a terrific fix for kicky dolls and dolls with "crazy legs." Another shout-out to PamSD of Dollovely for this simple technique. Try this before restringing!

Sueding is an absolute must for Peak's Woods Fairies of Color. They will stand for hours with their legs sueded.

Supplies

- Sharp scissors

- Dr. Scholl's Moleskin Plus (self-adhesive microsuede available at Target)

Technique

Do try this technique-- it really is simple, and it makes all the difference in your doll's ability to stand and hold a pose.

I suede my doll's hips, knees, ankles, shoulders, elbows and neck. You may want to remove your doll's head for sueding the neck joint, but you should be able to complete this technique without restringing.

The moleskin adheres to the socket part of your doll's joint. We'll suede half of the joint at a time.

1. First, cut a half-circle about the size of the joint you want to suede.

2. Then, cut pie slices from the center of the circle nearly to the edge of the circle, but don't cut all the way to the edge. This way, the moleskin will lie flat in the the socket.

3. Remove the adhesive backing and adhere it to the inside the socket, being careful not to block the canal through which the elastic runs, and keeping the moleskin below the edge of the socket (so it isn't visible on the outside).

4. Repeat with another half (or quarter) circle, as needed, until the socket has even coverage. Then, allow the ball to fit back into the socket, and it will push the moleskin into place. You'll see the difference immediately.

If you don't like the effect, you can easily peel off the moleskin and cut smaller or larger pieces, as desired. It doesn't leave residue and is easily removed.

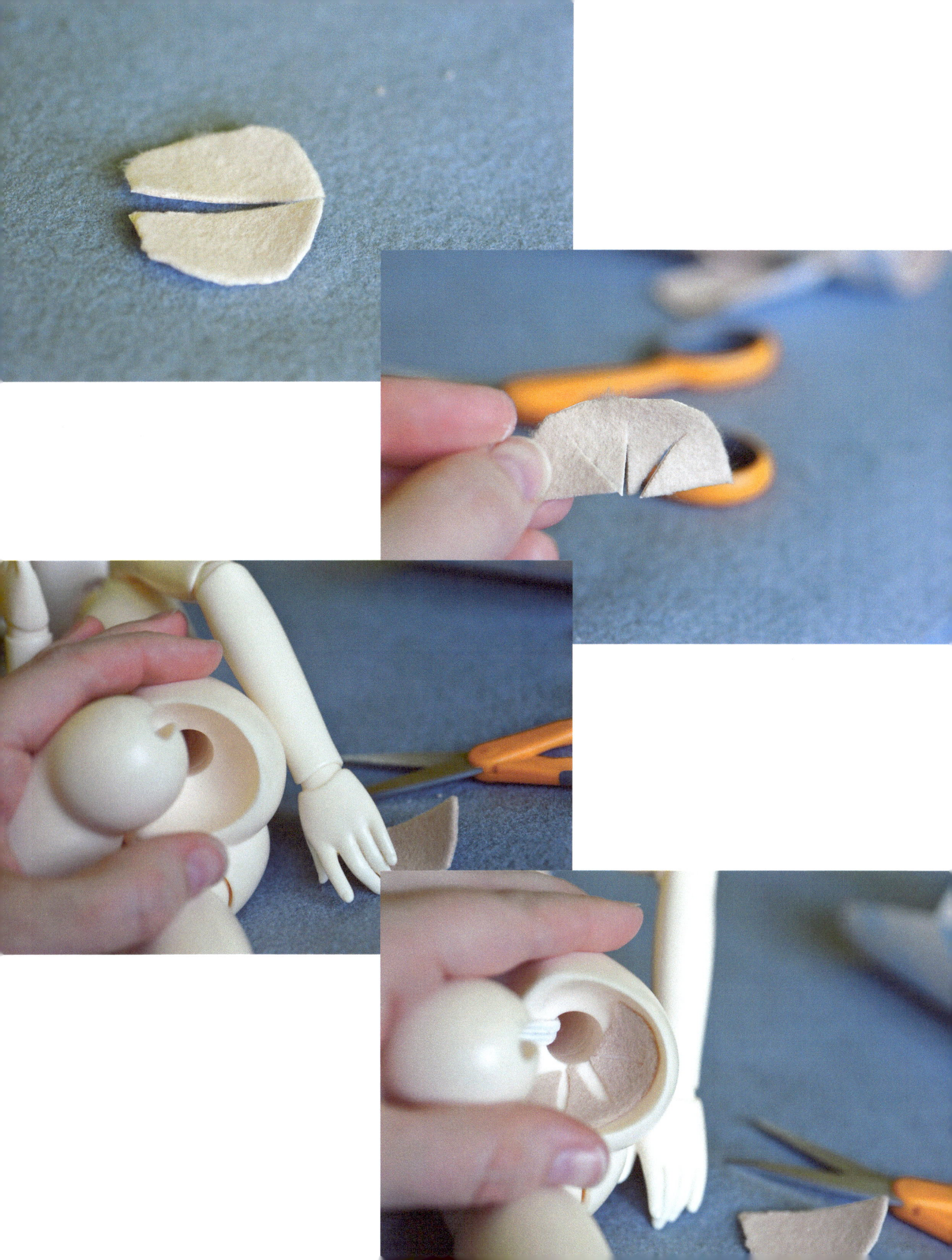

Sanding seams and smoothing resin

Use this technique to remove the seam lines in resin, small scratches and dents in your dolls, or do minor modifications to your doll's mold.

An important note before we start: If your doll is a tan or dyed resin, you will want to leave the seam lines alone. Colored resin may be tinted unevenly, or your doll might be dipped (so sanding will leave marks). Either way, I don't recommend sanding colored resin.

Supplies

- Wet wash cloth
- Bowl of water
- Dry lap towel
- Face mask
- Jewelry-grade sanding paper: 220, 440 and possibly 600 grit
- Mr. Superclear UV Cut (optional)

Technique

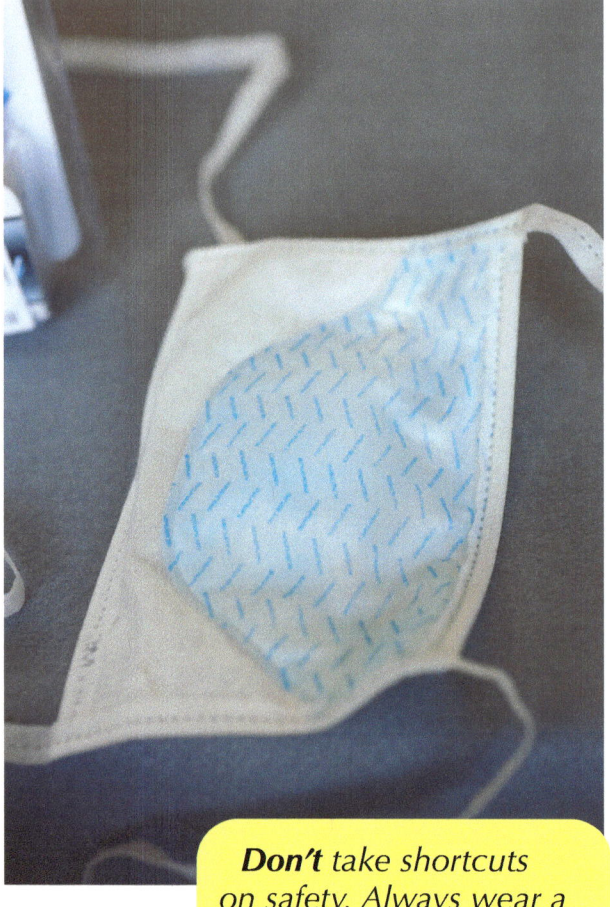

Don't take shortcuts on safety. Always wear a mask when you're working with resin dust. It's toxic!

Start by removing your doll's head. You won't want to mess up your doll's face-up while using this technique.

1. Put on the face mask. Using the sandpaper wet will help decrease the resin dust, but you must wear a mask, so you won't inhale even a little resin. It's toxic. Don't risk it.

2. Wet down the first part of the doll's body--I usually start with the torso. Wet the 220 grit sand paper and find the parting line, usually on the doll's neck and side. Using a light to medium touch and small overlapping circles, move the sand paper along the seam line until you can't feel it with your fingers. Check your work by wiping the dust off the doll frequently and rewetting with the cloth.

3. Repeat on the other side, rewetting the doll and paper as needed. You don't need to soak the doll, just wetting down the sandpaper and doll is fine.

4. Next, move to the finer grade of paper, 440 grit, and repeat steps 2 and 3. This grade should take out the color difference between the line and the rest of the body. You may need to follow up with 600 grit, or let the doll rest for a day and see how she looks in the morning to see the full results.

5. Do one piece at a time, careful not to accidentally modify any joints or to press too hard, especially with the coarser grits of sand paper.

6. When working on the hands and feet, take care not to damage the fingers and toes.

7. When you're finished, let the doll rest at least 24 hours, and look at your work in daylight. The lines should be the same color as the doll, even if you can't feel a raised line. If they aren't, it means you should sand a little more. Start again with 220 and work up to the finer grades of paper.

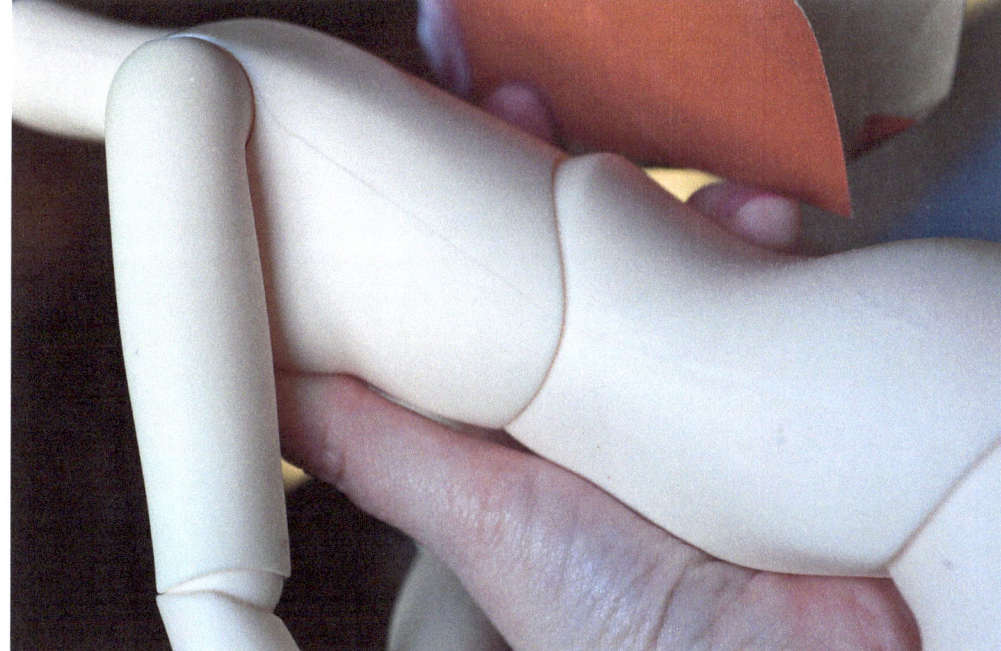

8. You can also consider blushing the doll with white or resin-colored pastels to cover any shade differences.

Once you're pleased with your results, and the doll has rested at least 24 hours, you have the option to spray her with a thin coat of Mr. Superclear UV Cut. Make sure you're using a fresh, well-shaken can, and that you spray outdoors (in a well ventilated area).

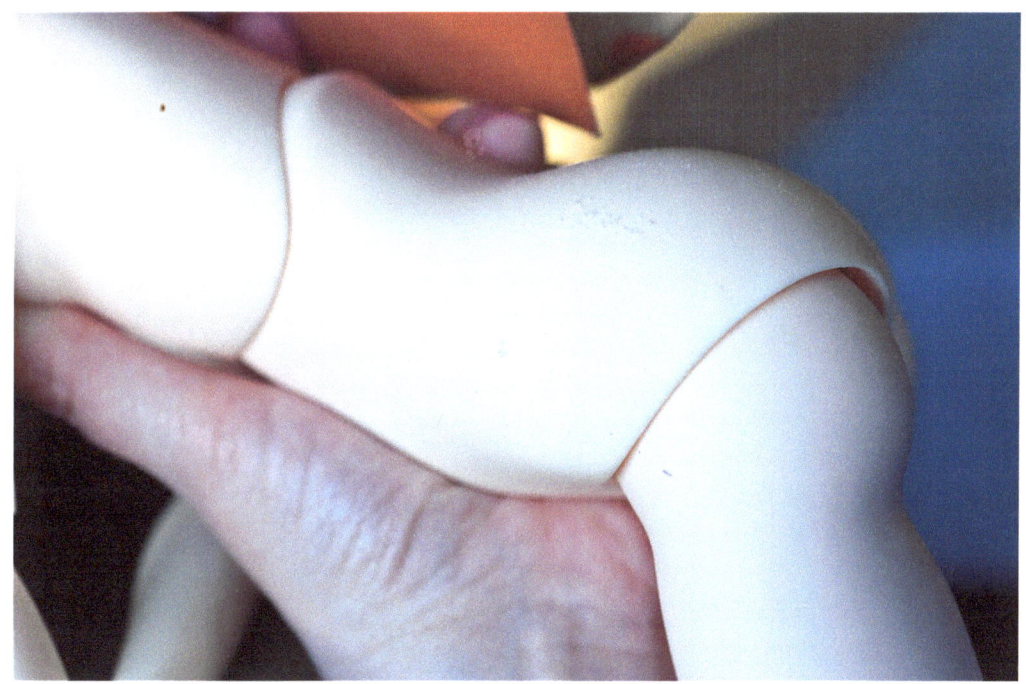

This gives your doll an extra coat of protection from light and dirt, and also primes her for body blushing.

Restringing

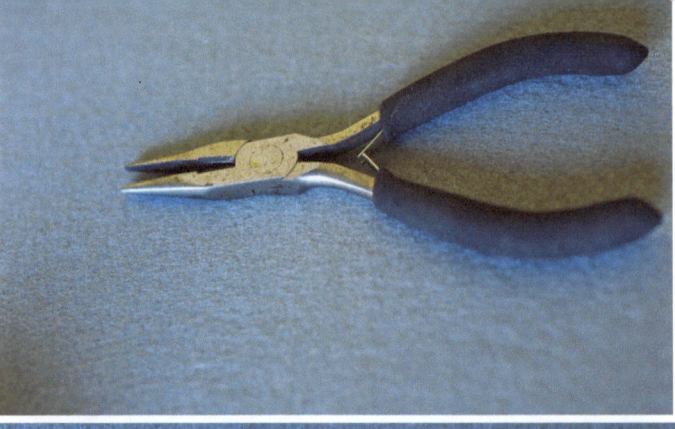

Depending on how long you keep your BJD, you may have to restring her at some point. If you buy a pre-loved doll, you may want to restring her when she arrives. This helps fix a lot of posing issues, and having fresh elastic is a great way to start.

Removing the head

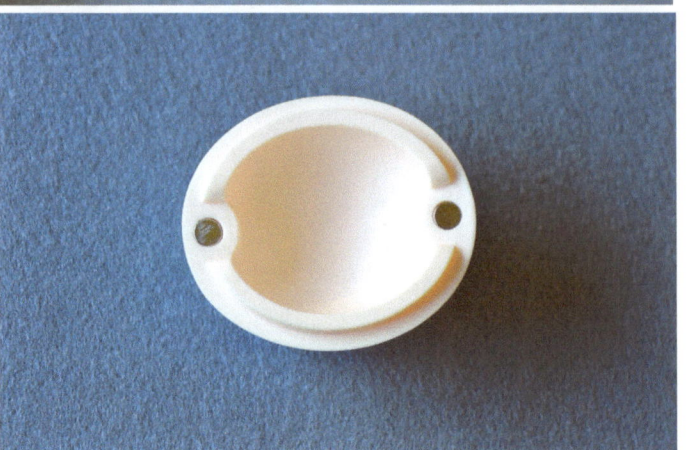

Most companies make it easy to remove your doll's head.

Supplies

- Pliers
- Pipe cleaner
- Hemostats (optional) or chopstick or unsharpened pencil

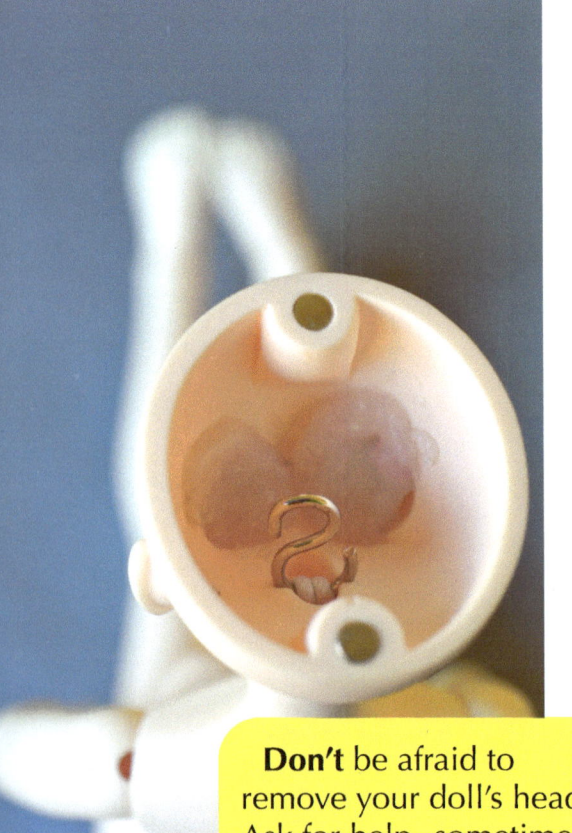

Technique

1. First, remove the doll's wig.

2. Your BJD will either have a head cap or a faceplate. Remove either the head cap or the faceplate and set aside.

3. Inside, you will find a hook and elastic. The hook will either be an S shape, or an O- or D-ring. Either way, using the pliers, turn the hook sideways 90 degrees. You can loop a pipe cleaner around the hook and grab it instead of the hook if it's hard to pull.

4. This will allow you to slip the hook (with elastic loops still attached) through the slot in the neck hole.

5. If your doll has an O-ring, you'll want to grab the elastic loops below the ring to prevent the ring from slipping down the neck (and the doll from becoming unstrung) at this point. I recommend using a pair of hemostats, but a single chopstick or pencil slipped through the ring above the neck hole will also do the trick.

Now that the head is removed, you can continue your work.

Don't be afraid to remove your doll's head. Ask for help--sometimes an extra pair of hands is the cure!

Unstringing the doll

Your BJD is strung with two elastic loops: one is strung through the torso and is held in place by the hand parts, and the other loop is threaded doubly through neck and is held in place by an S-hook (or O-ring) and both foot parts.

Before you unstring your doll, it's a good idea to label the pieces right and left with a pencil if it isn't obvious how the pieces go together. You can also take a picture of the pieces, but labeling is a safer method. This way, you won't have to restring your doll a dozen times to get the pieces right.

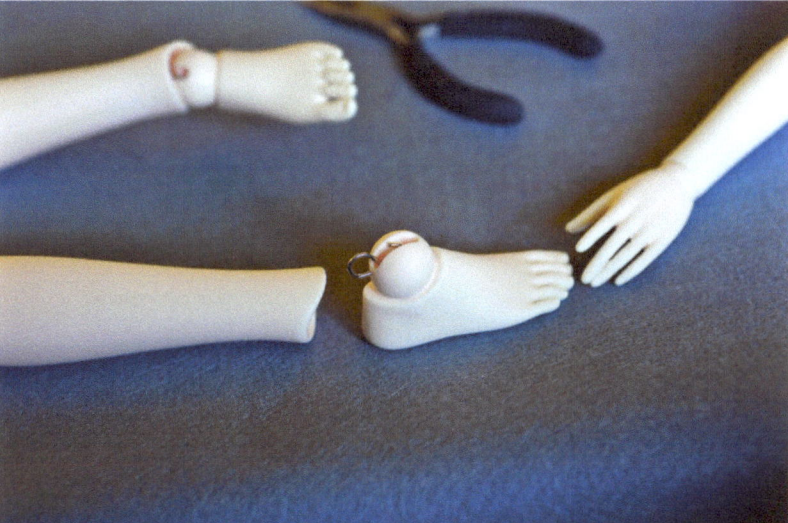

1. After removing your doll's head, carefully unhook both feet from the elastic. This should loosen the elastic loop that is strung through the neck.

2. Next, remove both hands from the elastic. Be sure to take extra care if your doll has resin hooks on the hands or feet. These can be delicate, so use hemostats to hold the elastic if you feel as if you're putting excessive pressure on them.

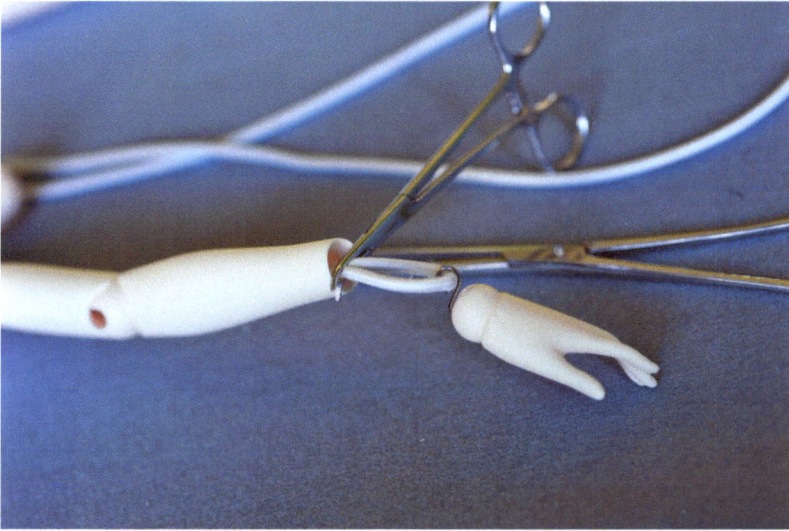

3. Now, you should be able to pull off the pieces of the arms and legs.

4. Finally, pull out the two loops of elastic.

Some companies string their dolls differently: Bobobie, for example, ties the two strings together in the torso. I've found that using two separate loops of elastic in their dolls works equally well. In fact, using a less stretchy elastic cord (one with a slightly larger circumference) and sueding the joints helps them to stand better, too.

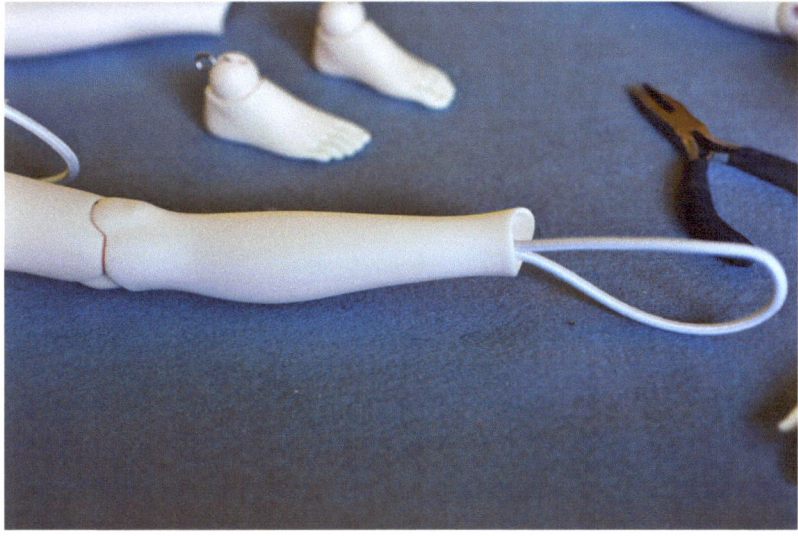

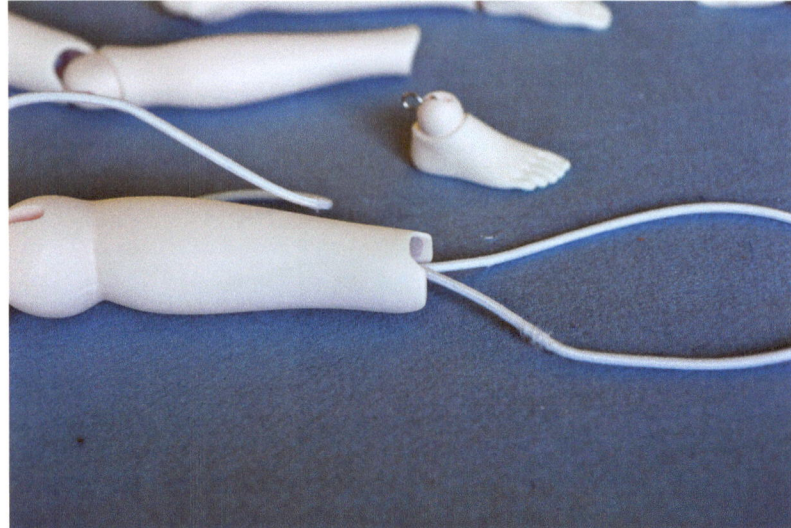

Elastic isn't expensive and is obtained easily. Size varies depending on the doll's height and the diameter of the canal inside the doll's legs and arms. Generally, I match the size I'm removing, buy extra from the company, or stick to these general rules:

70cm+ height: 5.5mm diameter

60-65cm: 4mm

60-30cm: 3.5mm (my standard)

20-30cm: 2.5mm

For dolls smaller than 20 cm, I have to see what the manufacturer used and usually buy extra. Some tinies take stretchy beading elastic, others use regular cord.

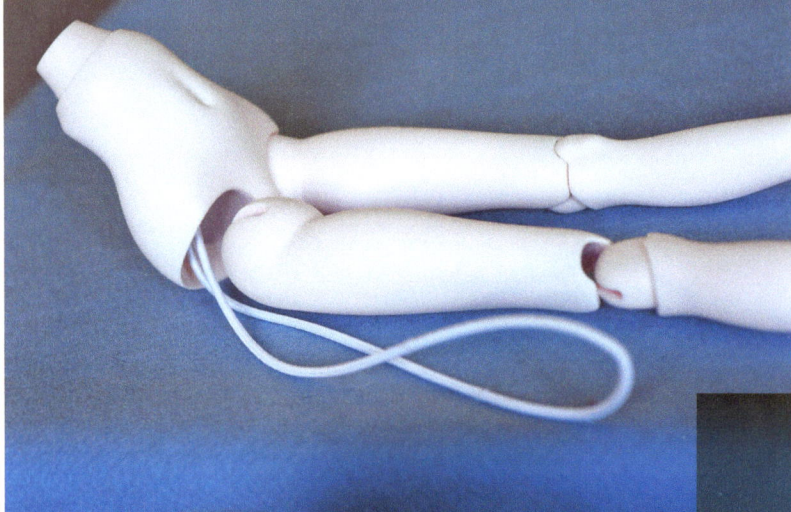

If your doll has an S-hook at the neck, you can carefully remove it for instant restringing. If your doll is strung tightly, however, the leg pieces may go everywhere, once this hook is removed.

This hook only holds the leg elastic in place. The arm elastic is tied in the center of the torso and is a separate loop.

The elastic you remove may still be in usable condition. Signs of wear include extra stretchy elastic, worn places in the elastic, or elastic that has been discolored or stretches unevenly. The torso elastic usually wears more slowly than the legs.

On the right, you can see the leg elastic is slightly worn in several places.

In the picture on the lower right, the arm elastic is still in good shape and in usable condition.

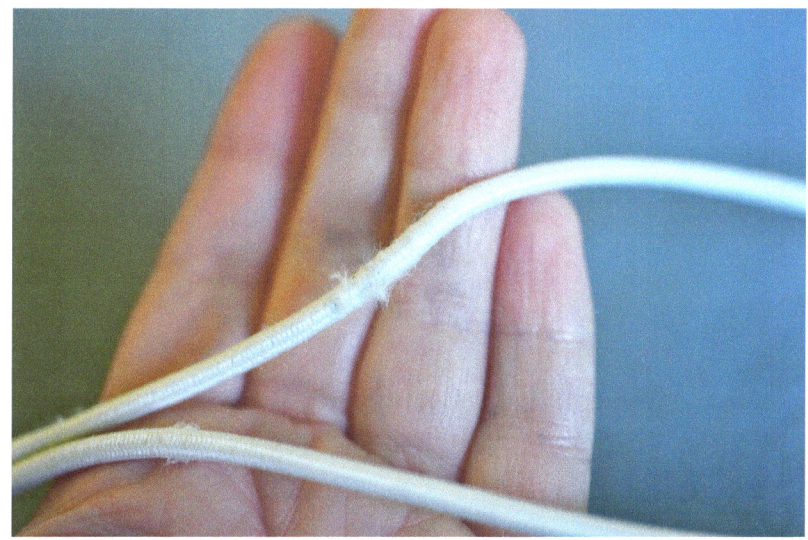

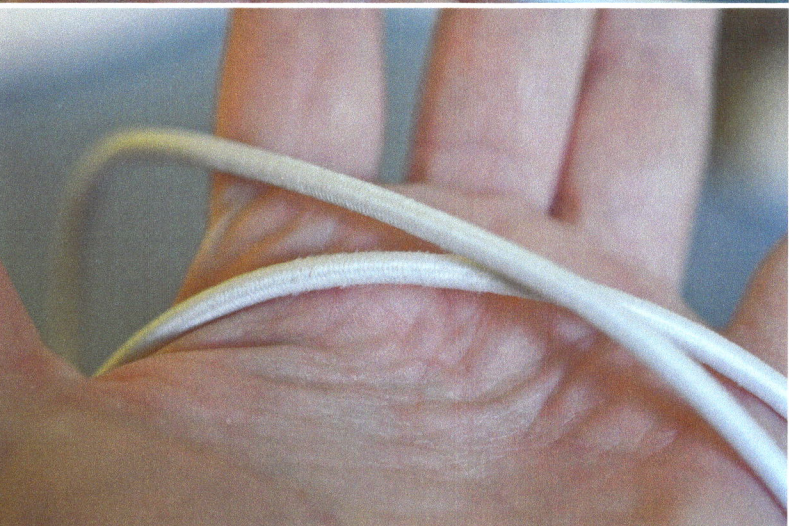

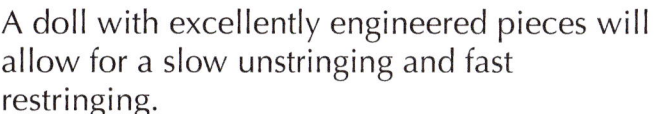

A doll with excellently engineered pieces will allow for a slow unstringing and fast restringing.

When the S-hook and torso parts are removed from a Peak's Woods, the knot (and folded-over loop) sit above the waist), while still keeping the legs intact. The feet and lower legs still remain together and strung, and aren't flying everywhere.

80

Restringing the doll, part 1 - the torso

Supplies

- Elastic cord
- Hemostats, at least one pair
- Chopsticks
- Stringing tool or pipe cleaner (if needed)
- Glass of wine or a legal chill pill (if needed)

Technique

Start with an unstrung doll. You've hopefully labeled the parts, so line them up where they should go now.

A note on tension: dolls that are strung too tightly can wear their joints down and chip them. Dolls that are too loosely strung won't stand or hold a pose. Perfect tension is a matter of practice, practice, practice.

If you are replacing elastic, the original loop will give you an idea of the length you need. Don't cut to size yet--keep in mind the original is stretchier than the new elastic, so you'll need to measure a *longer* length (by a few inches).

1. Make a loop with your untied elastic, and push the loop through the shoulder hole and down through the torso. If you need to use a stringing tool, use it. Push the tool through the shoulder, hook the elastic loop through the tool, and then pull the elastic through the arm. If you don't have a stringing tool, thread the loop with a pipe cleaner and push it through the hole.

> **Do** take take a break if you become frustrated. Stringing can be tricky the first few times, so take a breather if needed.

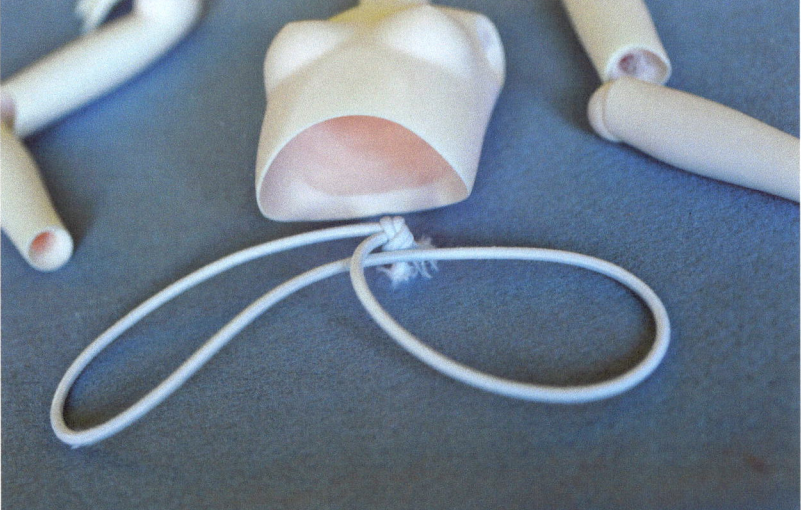
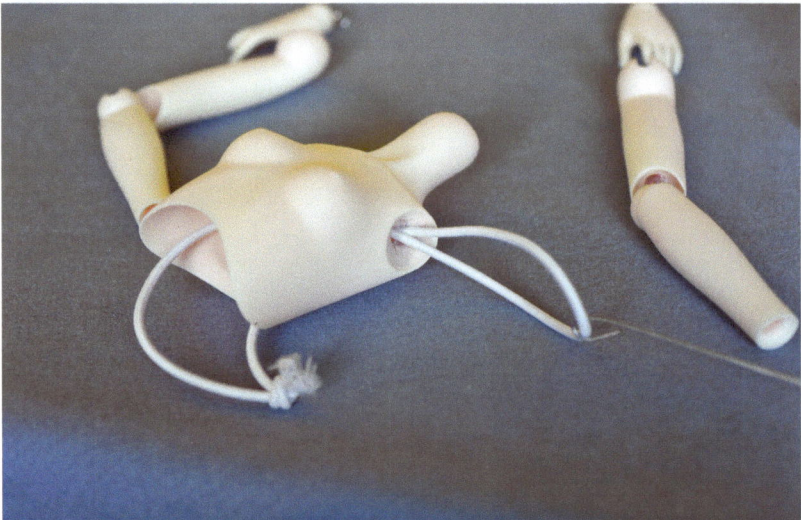
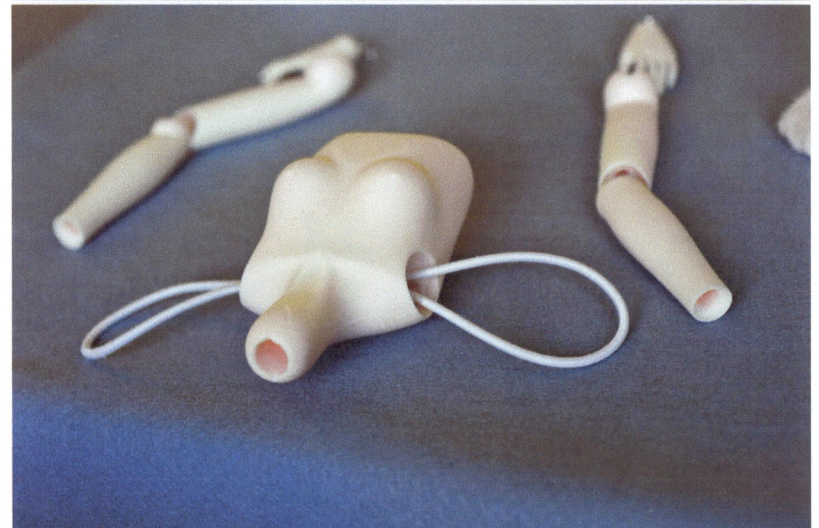

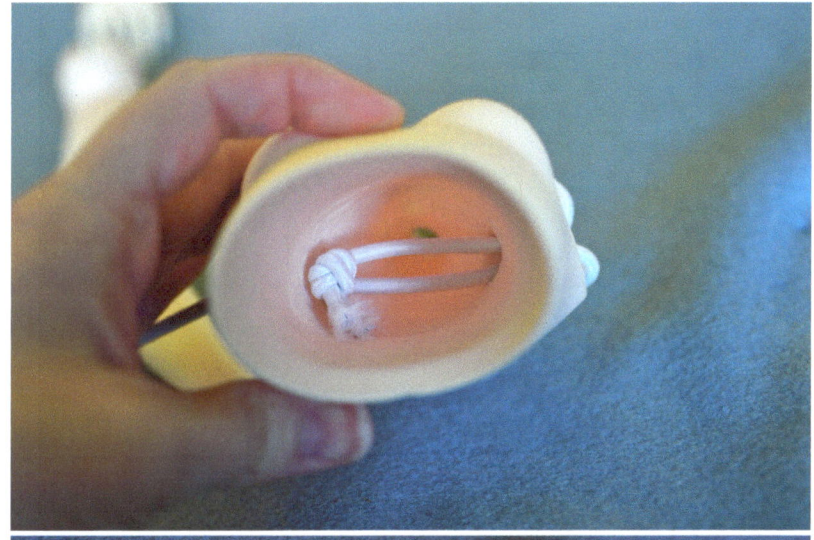

2. If you are using fresh elastic or if your doll has problems with arm posing, you'll want to keep the elastic knot outside of her torso for now. I usually keep the loop untied and clamped with hemostats at the shoulder. Otherwise, keep the knot inside the torso.

3. Now, push one side of loop through the upper arm. (Be sure you're using the right side.)

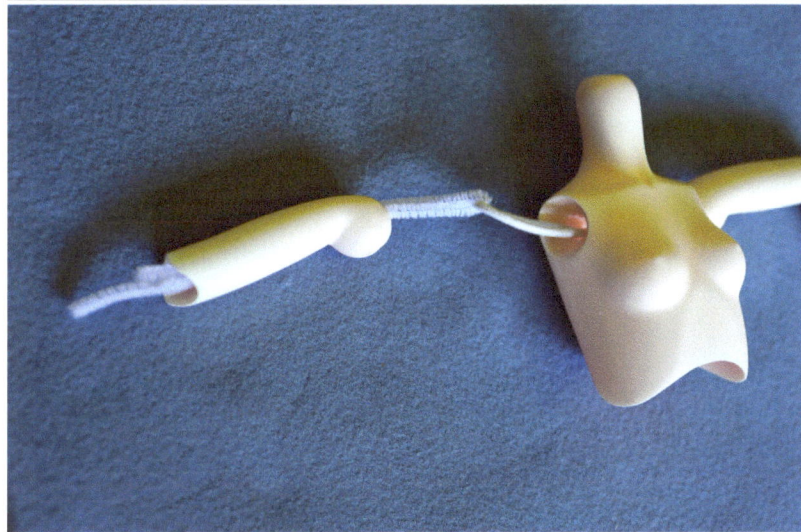

4. Next, thread the lower arm onto the elastic. If your doll is double-jointed, there will be another piece between these two pieces. Make sure they fit together before threading on the next piece.

5. Now, push the wrist joint (if there is one) onto the loop.

6. If you are using fresh elastic, use a chopstick as a placeholder for the hand. This will make it easier for you to adjust the tension. Otherwise, attach the hand.

7. On the opposite arm, continue as before, starting with the upper arm down the the hand. As before, if you're using fresh elastic and need to adjust the tension, use a chopstick instead attaching the hand.

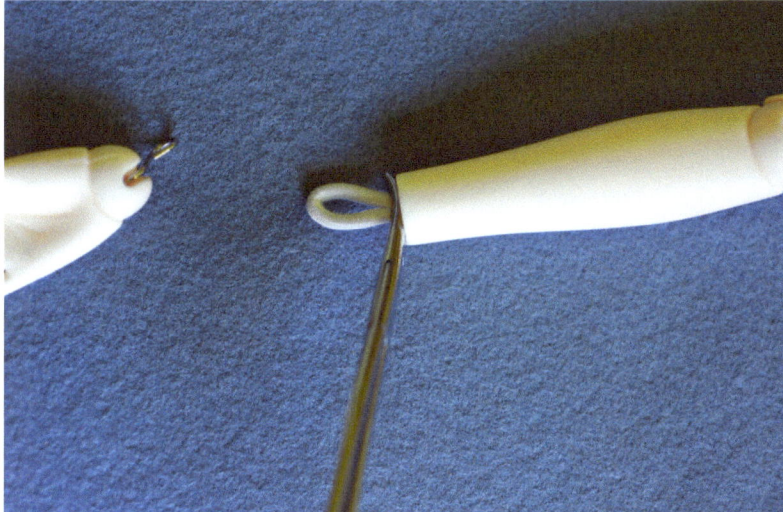

8. If your doll has no tension issues, you've just finished restringing your doll's torso! But if you notice your doll's arms won't stay posed above her head, you'll need to continue.

9. If the elastic knot isn't already outside of the torso, pull it through one of the shoulder holes, and untie it. Clamp both ends with a hemostat.

10. I use an "inchworm" method to adjust the tension. Basically, you'll be pulling only one side of the elastic to tighten.

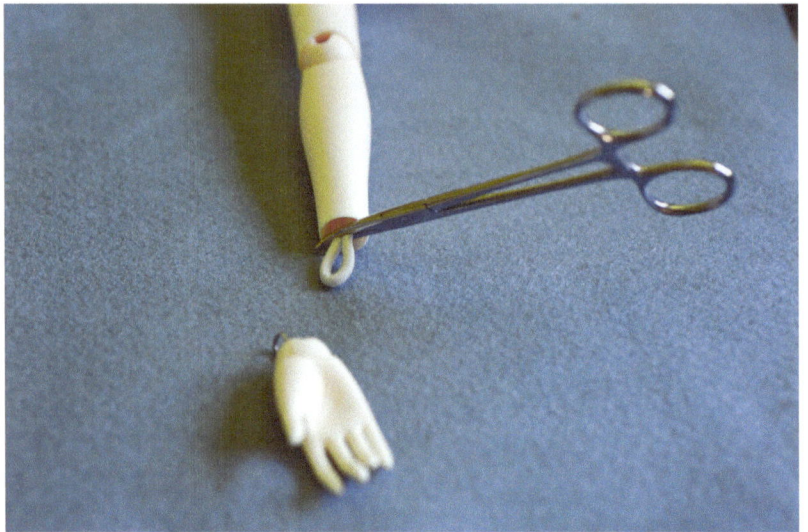

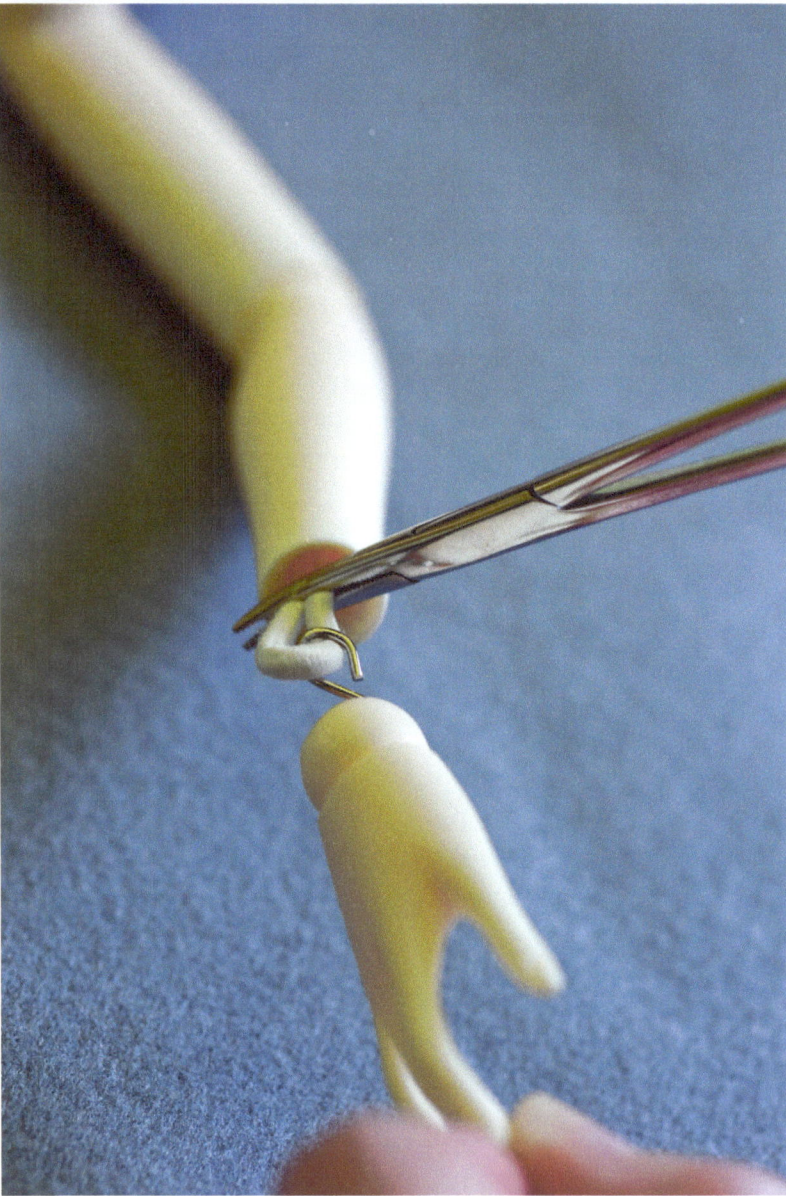

11. Keep one side of the elastic clamped with the hemostats to keep it from slipping.

12. Feed one side of the elastic through the entire length of the doll's stringing to tighten and then back up the other side. This is the most time-consuming part of restringing, but it will make a big difference in how your doll poses and feels to you.

13. Use a trial and error method to get a tension that feels right. A doll that is strung well will be able to hold a pose without feeling too kicky. A little kickiness is good--it's a sign of fresh elastic. Sueding joints helps this, too.

14. As soon as you have a tension that feels right, (Can she hold both chopsticks over her head and keep them there?) tie a knot. Surgical knots work well. Then, pull the knot back through the shoulder hole to the torso.

15. Trim off excess elastic, but leave a little extra at the ends, just in case you need to re-tie.

16. Now, attach the hands, carefully removing the chopsticks. If your doll has hands with wire hooks, you'll want to use the hemostats to hold the elastic while you hook them on. If your doll has resin hooks, be very careful not to snap the hooks off while stringing. Superglue can fix most resin breaks, but not hooks. They hold too much tension.

Restringing the doll, part II: the rest of the doll

Supplies

- Elastic cord
- Hemostats, at least one pair
- Chopsticks or two unsharpened pencils
- Stringing tool or pipe cleaner
- Glass of wine, or legal chill pill

Technique

You should already have the restrung torso of the doll (with arms and hands attached). Make sure you have the legs in the right order and ready to go--be sure all the pieces fit together perfectly, and are on the proper sides of the doll before you start.

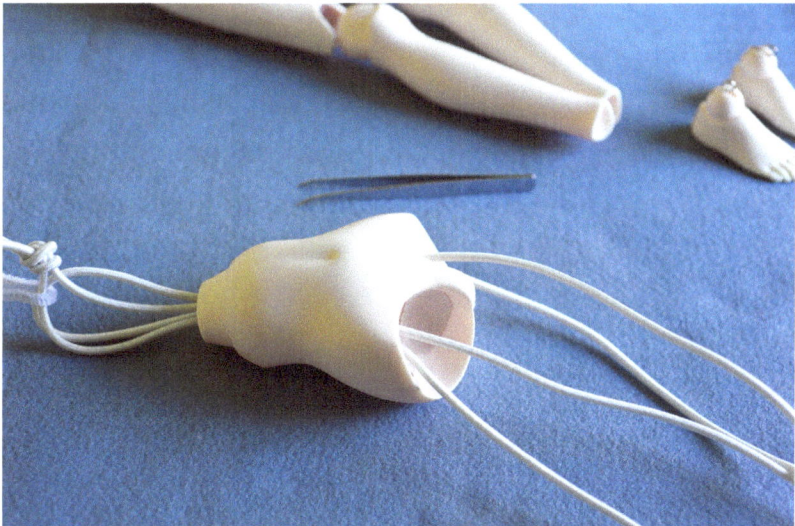

1. Estimate the amount of string you need. Add a few inches to the previous loop. It's easier to over estimate and trim later. Tie a temporary knot.

2. Thread one side of the loop through each leg opening. Check the photos before continuing. The loops should be equal lengths.

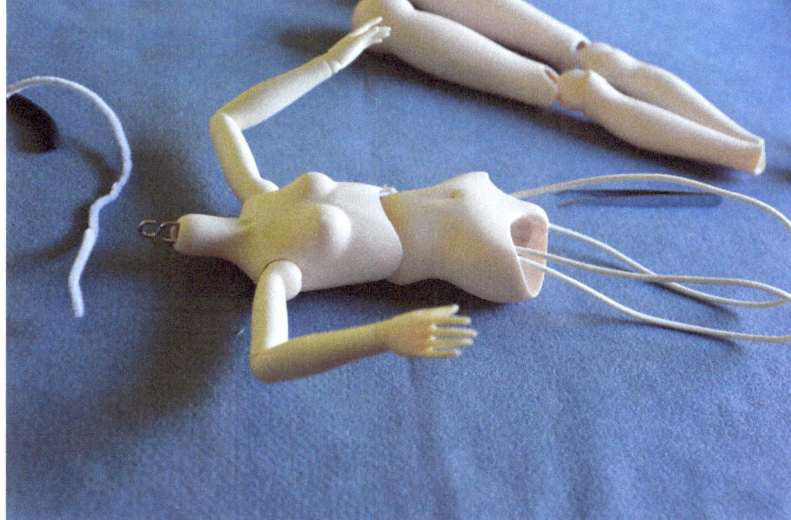

3. Using a pipe cleaner or restringing tool, pull the doubled loop through the torso through the neck. Hook over the top of the S-hook. The knot should be in the center of the torso. When you lay the pieces of the doll out and stretch the elastic over the top of them, they should be stretched, but not too tightly. Now is the time to lengthen or shorten your elastic. Make sure you even out the leg loops after tightening.

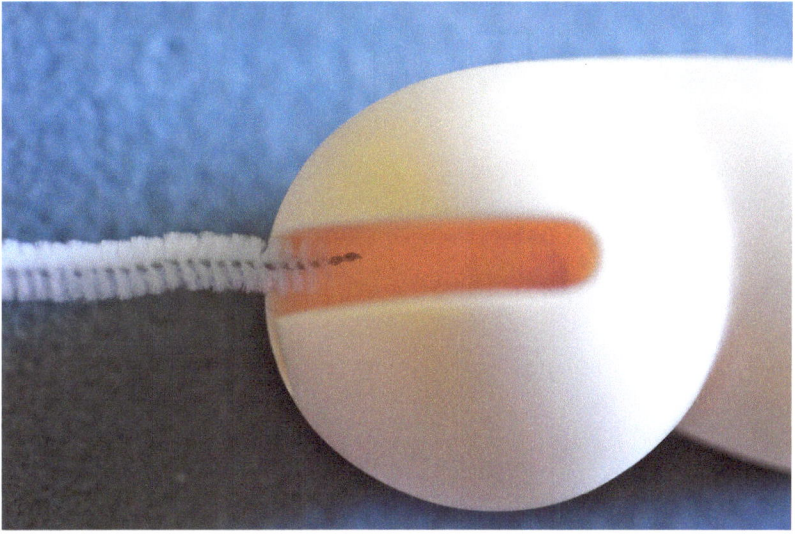

84

4. Next, thread the thigh pieces through the leg loops as shown. I'm using a pipe cleaner, but you can also use a stringing tool.

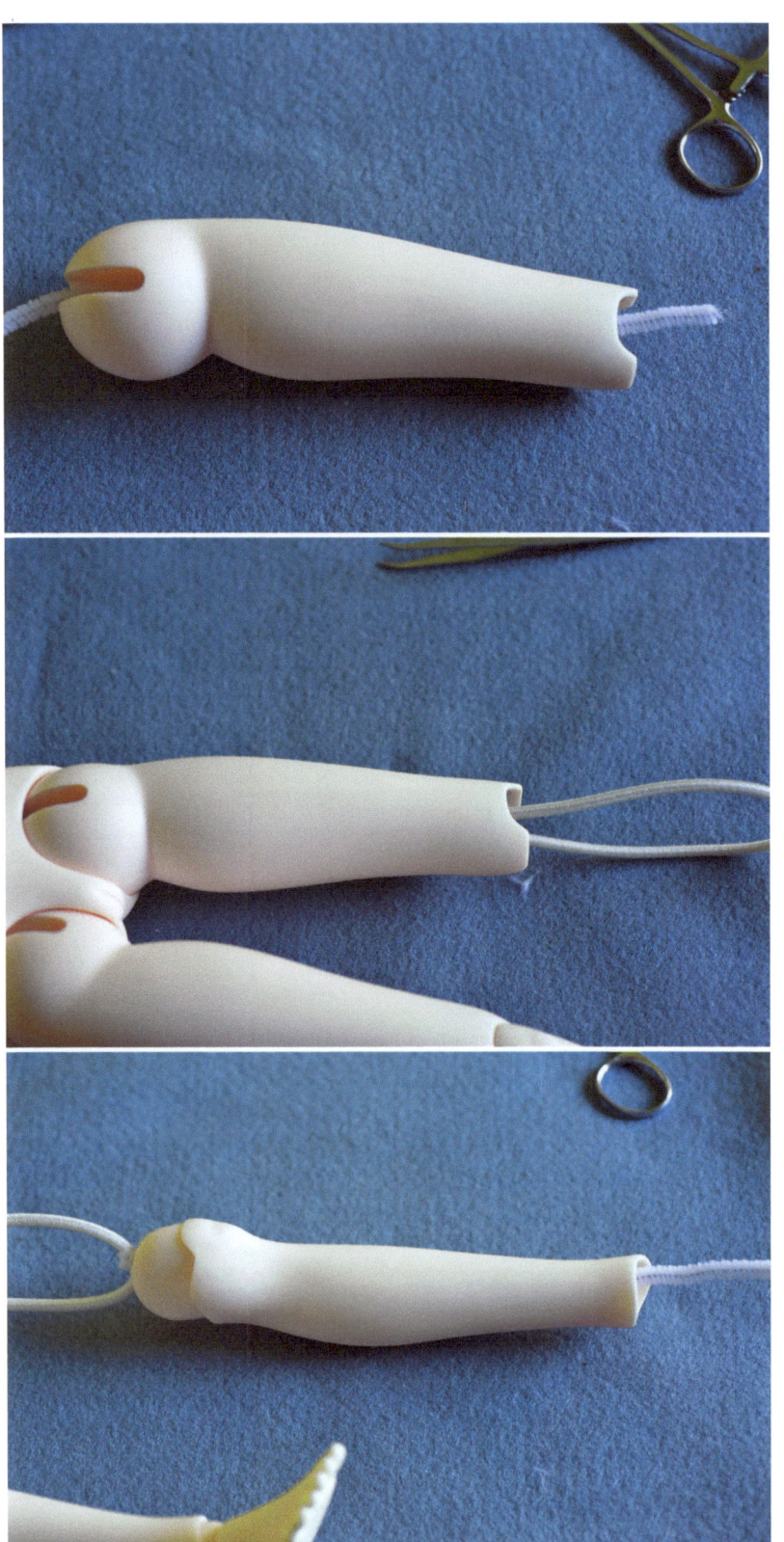

5. Thread the lower leg in the same manner. Don't forget the knee piece if your doll has double-jointed legs.

6. Next, string the ankle joint.

7. If the elastic appears to be tight enough, go ahead and hook on the foot next. Pay extra attention if your doll has resin hooks, such as those found in Iplehouse dolls. These can break if too much tension is put on them. Use a hemostat to hold the elastic in place while you hook the foot over the elastic.

8. If it looks like you've over- or underestimated the length of elastic, you may need to unstring the doll, retie the knot, then begin again.

You can also start restringing from the legs, and then pull the elastic up through the torso. If you can't get the elastic stringing correct on the third try, you can attempt this method. Tie the elastic *after* stringing the legs, estimating the length you'd need from the torso through the head joint. You might consider putting the feet on last in this case, and using chopsticks for place holders, since it's easier to adjust the tension around smooth, round surfaces than around metal hooks. Carefully replace the chopsticks (or pencils) with the doll's feet. Use hemostats if necessary.

A third option is to pull an untied loop through the top of the neck, along with the second loop. This way, you'll be able to tighten the doll's string through her neck, and adjust the tension in her legs more easily as the elastic wears. Keep in mind, however, that your doll's head must have a larger opening for the knot, so this isn't an option for all BJDs. Use the chopstick in her ankles until you have the tension equal in both legs, and don't hook her feet on until you're sure it's perfectly balanced on both sides.

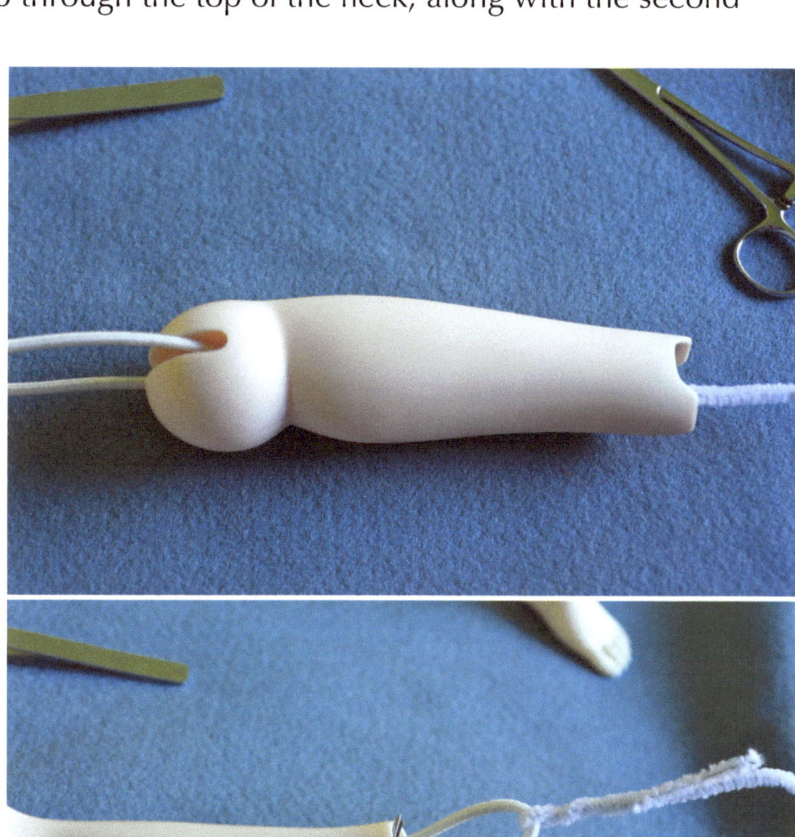

If you're using an O- or D-ring, you'll have to start the string from the neck. Feed the looped elastic down through the torso, with the ring at the top, and thread the elastic through the torso. Make sure the knot is tied in the torso of the doll before stringing the legs.

Congratulations! You've just finished restringing your doll. A special word of caution before we put your doll's head back on.

Because of the hand-cast nature of BJDs, you'll want to take extra care while restringing your doll and when using metal tools around resin. You might be surprised how easily (and loudly) the elastic snaps each resin piece to another as you're trying to get a pair of hemostats or pliers (or fingers-- ouch!) out of the way. My advice is to not let your doll's resin snap together, if you can help it.

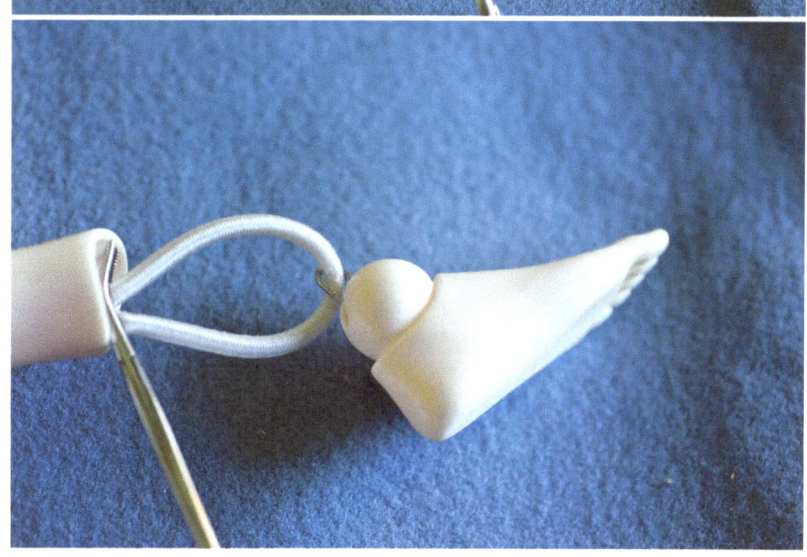

Instead of snapping the parts together, try holding the doll between your legs and then lowering the pieces back in place. Or, get a friend's pair of hands involved, so you can remove the metal tools safely.

In the photo on the left, you can see inside an older torso piece, which has been worn thin. It seems nearly transparent, ready to break. The light seems to shine right through it--imagine what an accidental stab with a pair of metal plier would do.

So what about that S-hook and the neck joint? I have a sneaky trick for you next.

Replacing your doll's head

Supplies

- Pliers

- Pipe cleaner

Nothing is quite as exciting as replacing your doll's head, especially when she has fresh elastic. It can be a little tricky, so you can try this technique.

Technique

1. Holding your doll between your knees, loop a fresh pipe cleaner through the ring or under the hook.

2. Thread the pipe cleaner through your doll's neck joint, and rest it on the neck. Hold the head gently by the ears.

3. Grab the pipe cleaner with your pliers and pull the hook straight up with one hand.

4. With your other hand, gently turn the head 90 degrees, so the hook can rest in the slot inside the doll's head.

5. Gently lower the pliers and remove the pipe cleaner.

6. Now exhale and relax.

If you let go while you're holding the pliers, you risk snapping the metal hook against your doll's resin head. It can leave dents inside the doll, and depending on the stringing, it could crack your doll. Plus, the metal pliers you're using might also damage the doll. Hold gently, turn the doll's head gently, and only after it is free of the metal hook. Then *lower* the hook gently--don't drop it.

Using a pipe cleaner gives you something to grip, it's easier to handle than a metal hook, and it gives you just a bit of leverage, right when you need it.

Enhancing projects

Feeling brave or artistic? Even if you aren't, you should give these projects a try. I highly recommend everyone try body blushing at least once. You don't have to seal it if you don't like the results.

Basic body blushing

Adding body blush enhances a doll's body sculpt and is an easy way to make your BJD more realistic. The technique is straightforward: add several shades of pastels to the valleys of the body and blend.

Supplies

- Mr. Superclear or Testors
- Chalk pastels
- Large round brush (size 6) and a small angled brush (size 1/8)
- Magic Eraser

Technique

Before you begin, remove your doll's head. Gently clean the body using a Magic Eraser. Make sure she is free from stains. I recommend sanding seam lines before blushing.

1. Prime the doll by spraying her with sealer. Make sure you have plenty of ventilation, following the directions on the can. I walk around the doll, using a light coat to prevent flagging (dripping). Let dry, and repeat on the doll's other side.

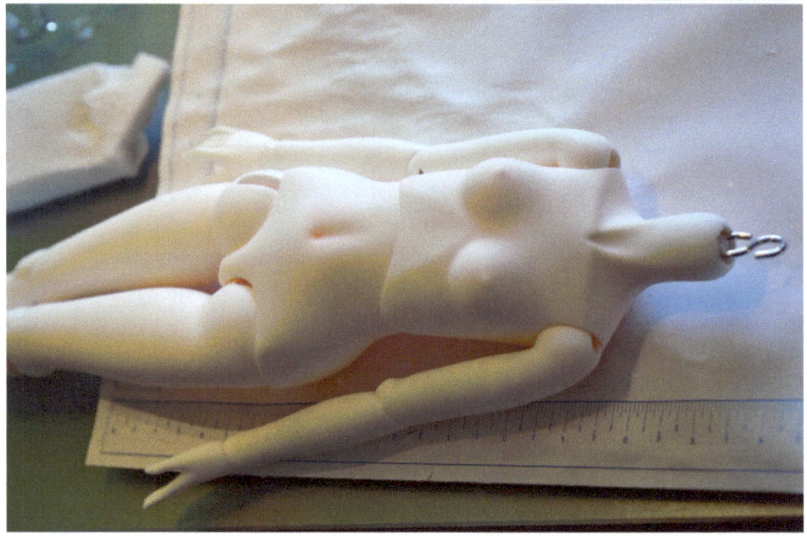

2. Choose the color palette based on the doll's face-up. I use three or four colors: white for blending, a color just a shade darker than the doll's skin tone, one close to the doll's cheek color, and one that is similar to her lip or eyeshadow color. I make a palette on scrap paper and blend them.

3. To apply, begin with the color closest to her skin tone. I start at the torso. Remember, you're only applying color to the dips (valleys) in her body. Using the angled brush, apply a bit of the color to her belly button, and blend with the large round brush.

4. Repeat with the next darkest shade, working in layers, blending each layer as you go. You don't have to use the darkest shade in every area. If you add too much, just wipe Magic Eraser over the doll to remove chalk from the raised areas.

5. As you can see from my finished photos, I apply blush to joints also, but the effect is very subtle.

6. You can also simply blend all the colors together, and apply a single shade in multiple layers. You will get a similar effect with less effort.

7. Spray the doll with resin sealer when finished, making sure to spray in the joints as well. Use a light coat and dry thoroughly before spraying the other side.

If your doll has dramatic face paint, you might prefer more dramatic blushing. You can get that effect by adding additional layers or using darker colors.

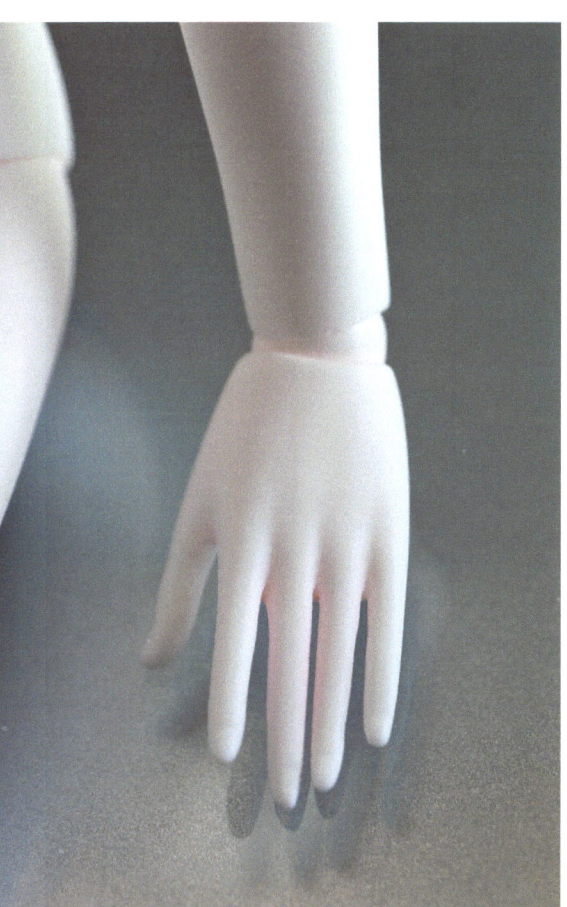

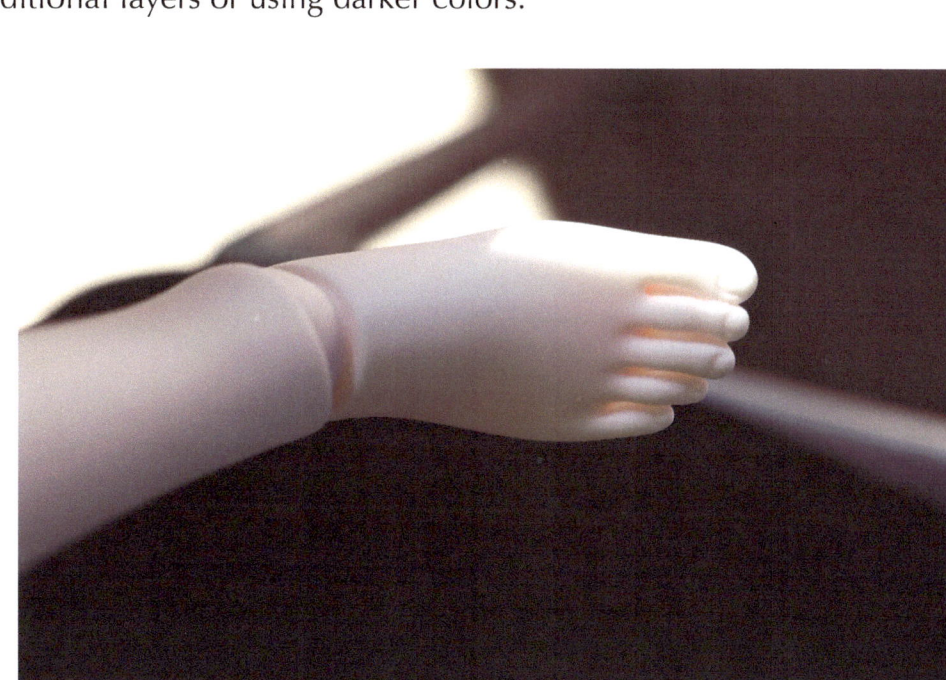

Adding a French manicure or pedicure

This technique works well with resin BJDs or vinyl dolls. Start with a clean, blushed and sealed BJD.

Supplies

- Sharpened water color pencils (white, maybe pink or nude also)
- Very fine brush (#1) or toothpick
- Liquitex gloss medium or Tamiya X-22 gloss

Technique

If the doll is small, you'll only need the white pencil. For larger dolls, you may want an additional shade.

1. For toes, drag the side of the white pencil along the edge of the toenail. To add more dimension, add a bit of pink or nude to the base of the nail bed.

2. For hands, repeat step 1. Use the sculpt of the nails as your guide. Wipe off any excess with a paper towel. Remember, this is a watercolor pencil, so it will wipe clean with water at this point. Add pink or nude to the base of the nail, if desired.

3. When you're happy with your results, seal the nails only with a thin coat with the gloss medium. Be careful not to drip on the rest of the doll. Use a toothpick if needed.

4. Let the gloss dry. Vinyl takes longer to dry than resin, so don't rush.

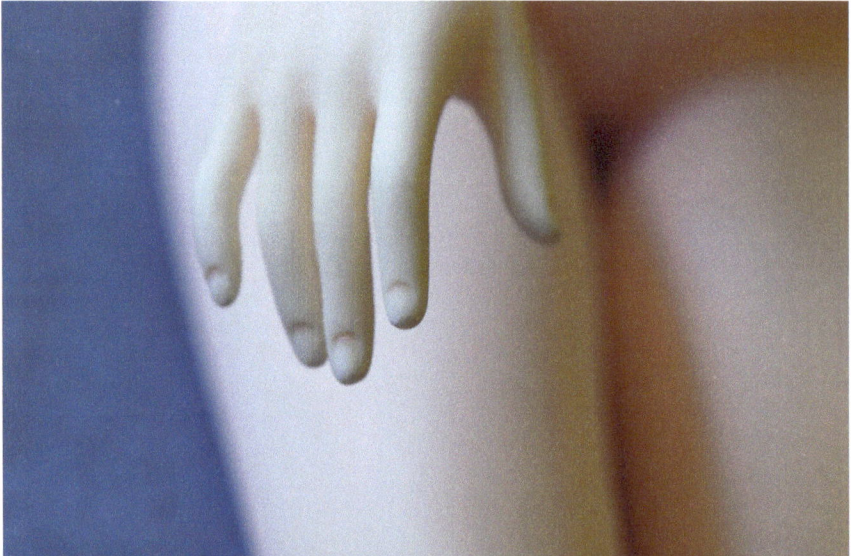
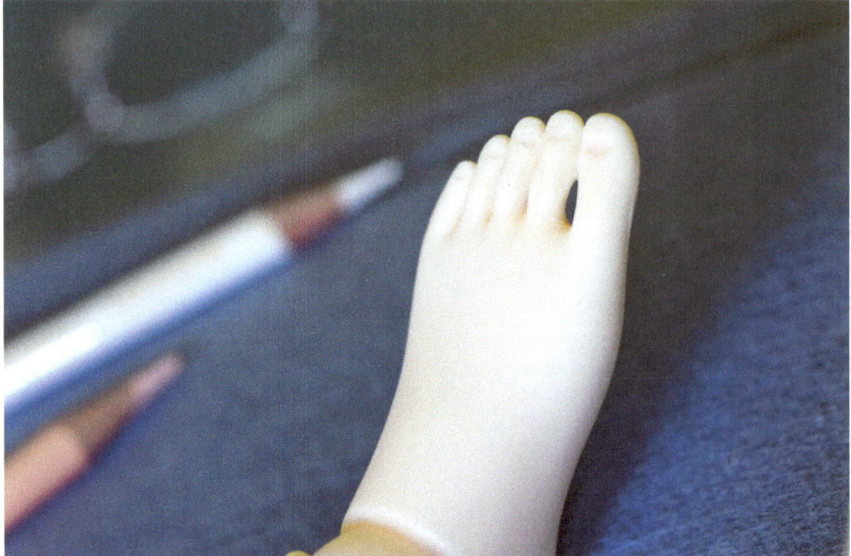

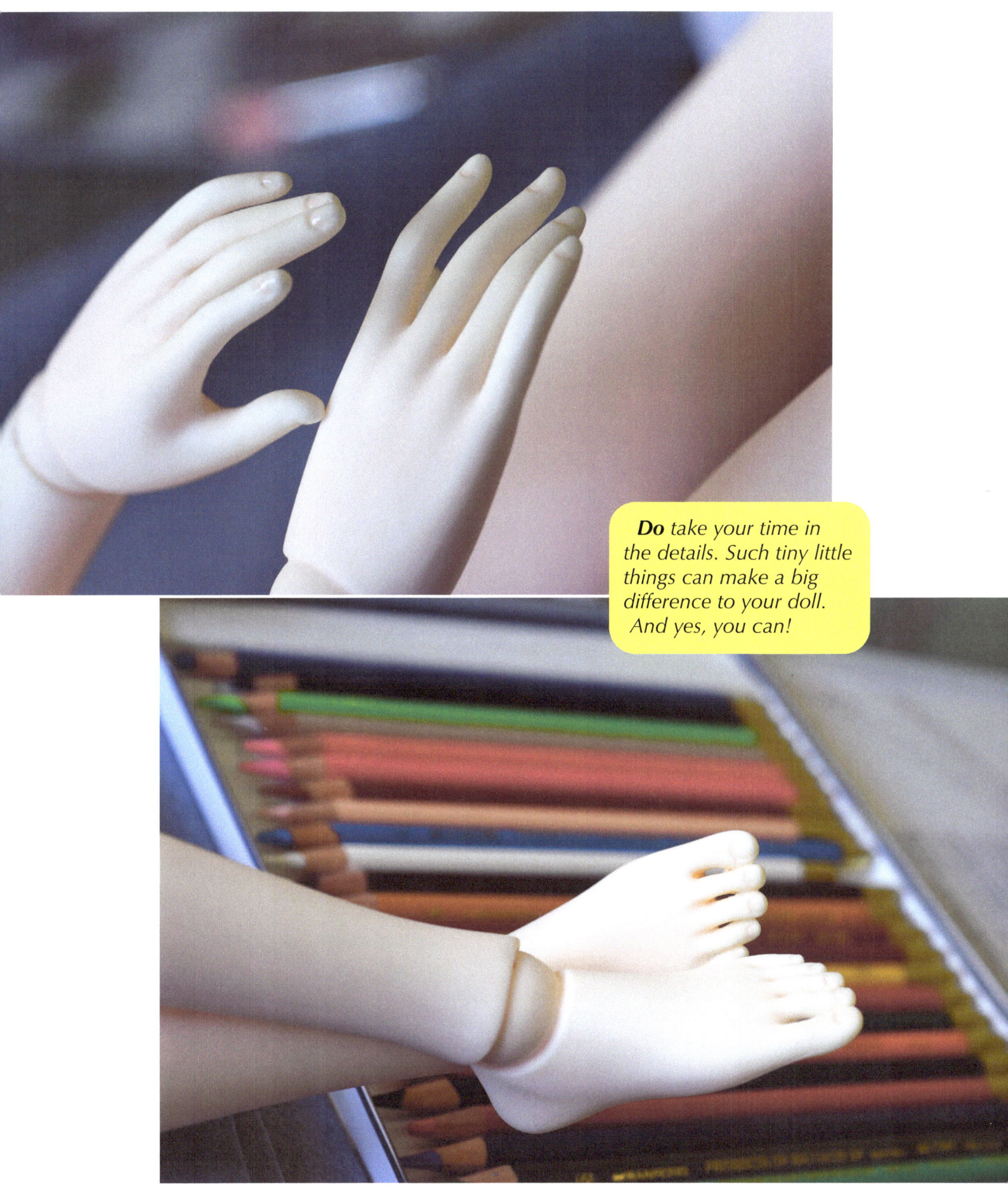

Do take your time in the details. Such tiny little things can make a big difference to your doll. And yes, you can!

Adding or repairing eyelashes

This is really a handy thing to know how to do. Some dolls do not include eyelashes when they are shipped from the company, and you may want to consider adding your own.

Supplies

- Aleene's Fast Grab Tacky Glue

- Tooth picks

- Eyelashes: I recommend using false eyelashes for humans, and cutting them in half. Audrey Hepburn style lashes--longer on the outside and tapered--are perfect. You can often find fun lashes at the dollar stores or discount stores in your neighborhood, especially around Halloween.

Technique

1. Remove your doll's head and eyes.

2. If your doll has eyelashes already, you might consider removing them. I usually keep my doll's undamaged lashes on, however, and use the new pair as "false lashes." To remove damaged lashes, use soapy water. Most companies use water-soluble glue to adhere lashes. If you use anything more harsh, you risk damaging the face-up, so be careful not to scrape or scratch the eye area.

3. Cut the eyelashes to the desired width. Human-sized lashes usually need to be cut in half for Peak's Woods dolls. Don't worry about the length for now. Try them on for size, and trim if needed before adding any glue.

4. Using a toothpick, apply a thin line of Fast Grab glue to the inner rim of the upper eye lid, just where you want the lashes to go. Don't use too much glue--remember, you can always add more.

5. Carefully insert the eyelashes, one eye at a time. The glue grabs instantly, but takes time to dry, so you have some time to place them just how you like. You'll notice that your doll will have a more sultry look if you aim the lashes down, and a wider-eyed innocent look if you aim them up.

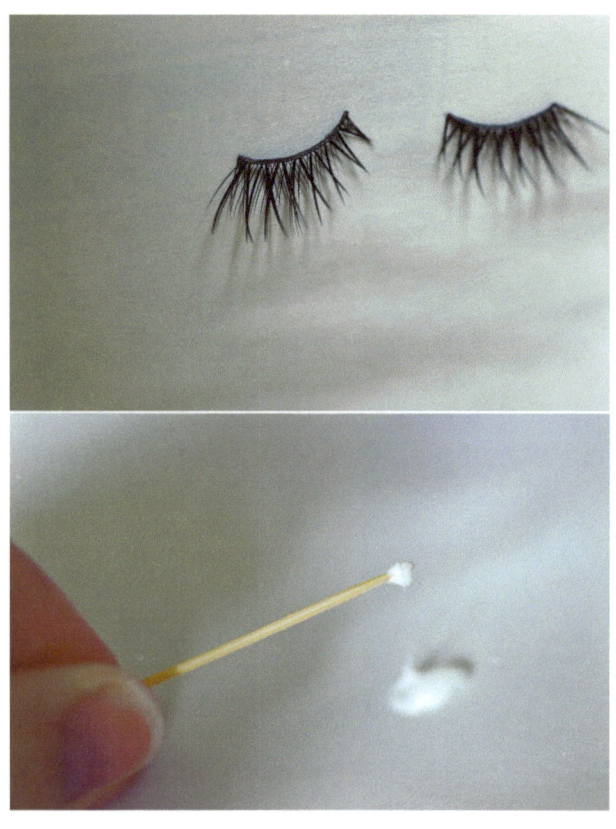

6. Use the other end of the toothpick for placement help. Be sure the entire edge of the lashes is sticking to the inner eye ridge.

7. Now, repeat on the other eye, making sure to match the first eye as best you can.

8. Let the glue dry thoroughly before you put the eyes back in. I suggest leaving the head out overnight to be safe.

You can use colored eyelashes, lashes with rhinestones, feathers, or only add a few super-long lashes on the outside corners of the eyes for different effects.

Plus, Aleene's is a water-based glue, which can be removed with water. You can easily try another pair for a fresh new look.

De-yellowing resin

For dolls that have significant or uneven yellowing, this technique will help even out their skin tone. This is a more extensive project, so you shouldn't start this the day before a doll meet.

If your doll has splotchy yellowed marks, this is a good fix. However, you might consider attempting to blush over those areas first. As long as her seam lines are sanded, you can almost always match a chalk pastel to the original skin tone, and even out your doll's skin perfectly with a much easier method.

Supplies

- Unstrung doll
- Acetone (no color)
- Cotton balls
- Protective eye gear
- Soft towels
- Sand paper (220, 400 and 600 grit)
- Magic Eraser cleansing sponge
- Face mask

Technique

1. Remove any moleskin sueding from the unstrung doll, if needed. Set the head aside, unless you plan to remove her face-up also.
2. One piece at a time, clean each piece of the doll with a quick rub of acetone. Use a fresh, clean cotton ball each time. Damp cotton balls will be enough to get the job done. Let each piece dry on a clean soft towel.
3. Do not soak the doll in acetone. Be sure to work in a well-ventilated area, and use eye protection.
4. Leave each piece to dry for at least 24 hours. Keep in mind acetone softens resin, and if you start sanding before the acetone has dried, you will risk damaging your doll.
5. The next day (or later), you'll start removing the yellow with sand paper. Again, work one piece at a time. Be sure to wear the mask at all times. Start with damp 220 grade paper, and a damp towel, and work in small concentric circles on the most yellow piece of the doll. Don't push hard--you're just trying to even out the skin tone. Use a gentle touch in small, circular motions.
6. Wipe off the resin dust using a wet rag and check your work regularly, as you did in sanding seam lines. Don't over sand edges or joints, as these will become thin and brittle, and may interfere with how the balls and sockets fit together later.

7. Keep in mind to look for thin or worn spots on the resin as you work. Hold the piece up to the light and check for any transparent areas. Don't sand those.

8. Move up to 400 grit paper, and then 600 if desired for a smooth finish on the doll. Finish with Magic Eraser if desired.

9. Move on to the next piece, making sure each color matches with the previous finished pieces.

10. When each piece is complete, let the entire doll rest 24-48 hours. If you're pleased with the color, restring the doll. If not, start sanding.

11. Finish by sealing with two coats of MSC UV cut for better protection.

Sometimes, only a doll's arms will have yellowed differently than the rest of the body. You can usually fix this without the use of acetone. It's my preference to avoid acetone when I can, and try sandpaper alone first.

Above on the right, you can see a before photo of poor stained Mintie. Her arms were probably exposed to light or perhaps a darker fabric for a prolonged period of time.

The photo below shows Mintie after the de-yellowing technique. Her arms are now closer to her body color.

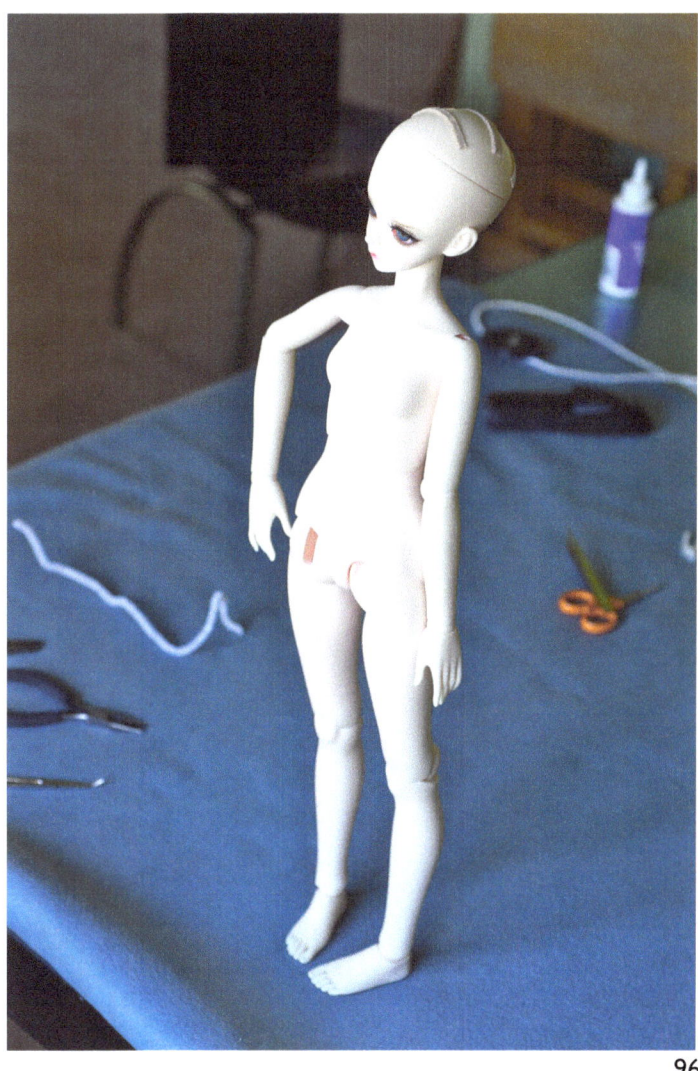

Easy sewing project for your new BJD

Here is a quick and easy sewing project for your new BJD, from Jen Eugley of JennyGrey Designs. You can sew this by hand or by machine, and change the length, add pockets or decorative buttons or lace, make a ruffled neckline and more.

These patterns are sized at 100% for large dolls (58 cm girls). A seam allowance of 1/4" is included.

Supplies

- fabric (knit for the leggings), enough to fit the pattern pieces
- thread
- needle
- scissors
- snaps or velcro
- 1/4" wide elastic

For Tunic

1. Cut two of TUNIC FRONT (one of fabric, one of lining) and four of TUNIC BACK (two of fabric, two of lining).
2. Cut a 2" x 25" piece of fabric for the bottom RUFFLE.
3. Sew shoulder seams of TUNIC FRONT to TUNIC BACK, with the right sides together. Press seams open.
4. Repeat step 2 with lining pieces.
5. Sew fabric to lining in the following steps:
    a. Up center back, around neckline, down other side of center back.
    b. Around each armhole.
6. Clip curves and corners.
7. Turn right side out by pulling back pieces through each shoulder opening. Press curved edges.
8. Sew front to back side seams together: from bottom hem of fabric, up to underarm, and back down lining side seam. Press seams open.
9. Fold over and press one long edge and both ends of RUFFLE about 1/8". Fold over again and top stitch.
10. Gather unfinished edge of RUFFLE with a basting stitch and sew (right sides together) to bottom hem of fabric only. Press seam allowance upward.

11. Fold over bottom edge of lining 1/4" and topstitch fabric to lining (sandwiching seam allowance between) 1/8" from where tunic body meets RUFFLE.

12. Overlap center back desired amount for a good fit. Topstitch from bottom hem along center back 3" up from bottom hem.

13. Add snaps or velcro to close the top.

For Leggings

1. Cut out one of LEGGINGS from knit fabric on center front fold.

2. Fold top over 1/2" and topstitch 3/8" from folded edge.

3. Thread 8-1/2" length of 1/4" wide elastic through waistband and topstitch at either end.

4. Sew center back seam, right sides together. Press open seam allowance and topstitch seam allowance down at top of waistband.

5. Fold bottom hem of each leg up 1/2" and topstitch 3/8" from folded edge.

6. Match front crotch to back crotch. Sew inseam (right sides together) from bottom hem, up one leg to crotch, then back down the other leg to bottom hem.

7. Clip crotch and turn inside out.

About stitching techniques

Are you brand new to sewing? Here are some helpful resources for beginning sewers(including different stitching techniques), specifically for BJD lovers:

http://www.dolldazzle.com

The Links page includes handy tips for measuring and fitting dolls, plus beginning techniques and links to other sewing and websites.

http://www.dalerae.com

Dale Rae not only carries an amazing array of shoes, hose, and patterns on her site, she also lists free patterns, sewing hints, and tutorials, specifically for doll (and ball-jointed doll) collectors.

http://www.gracefaerie.com

Easy-to-use patterns with great instructions, these are some of the finest available for BJD collectors. You can buy them from her list of dealers, and also find them already made from her Links list.

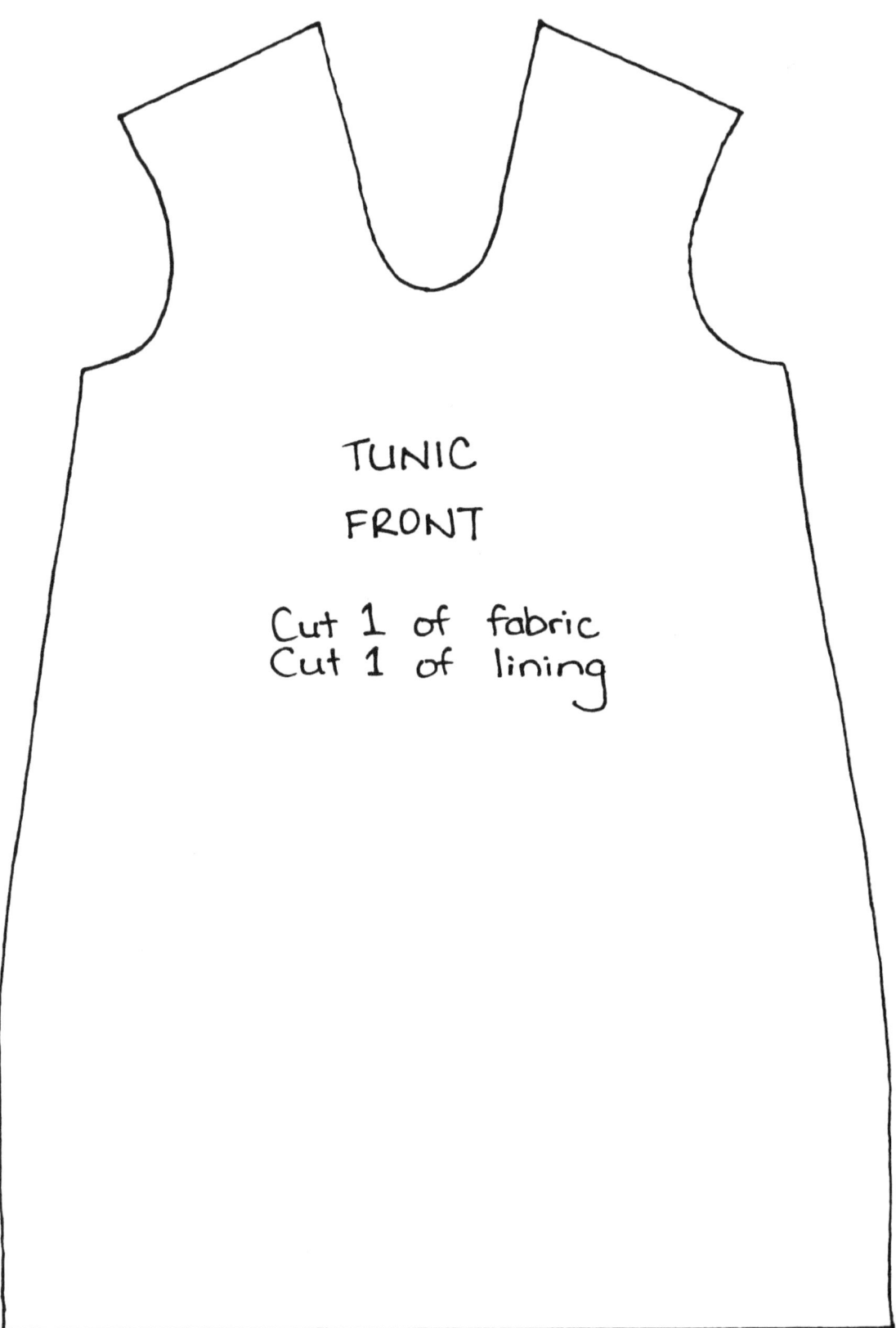

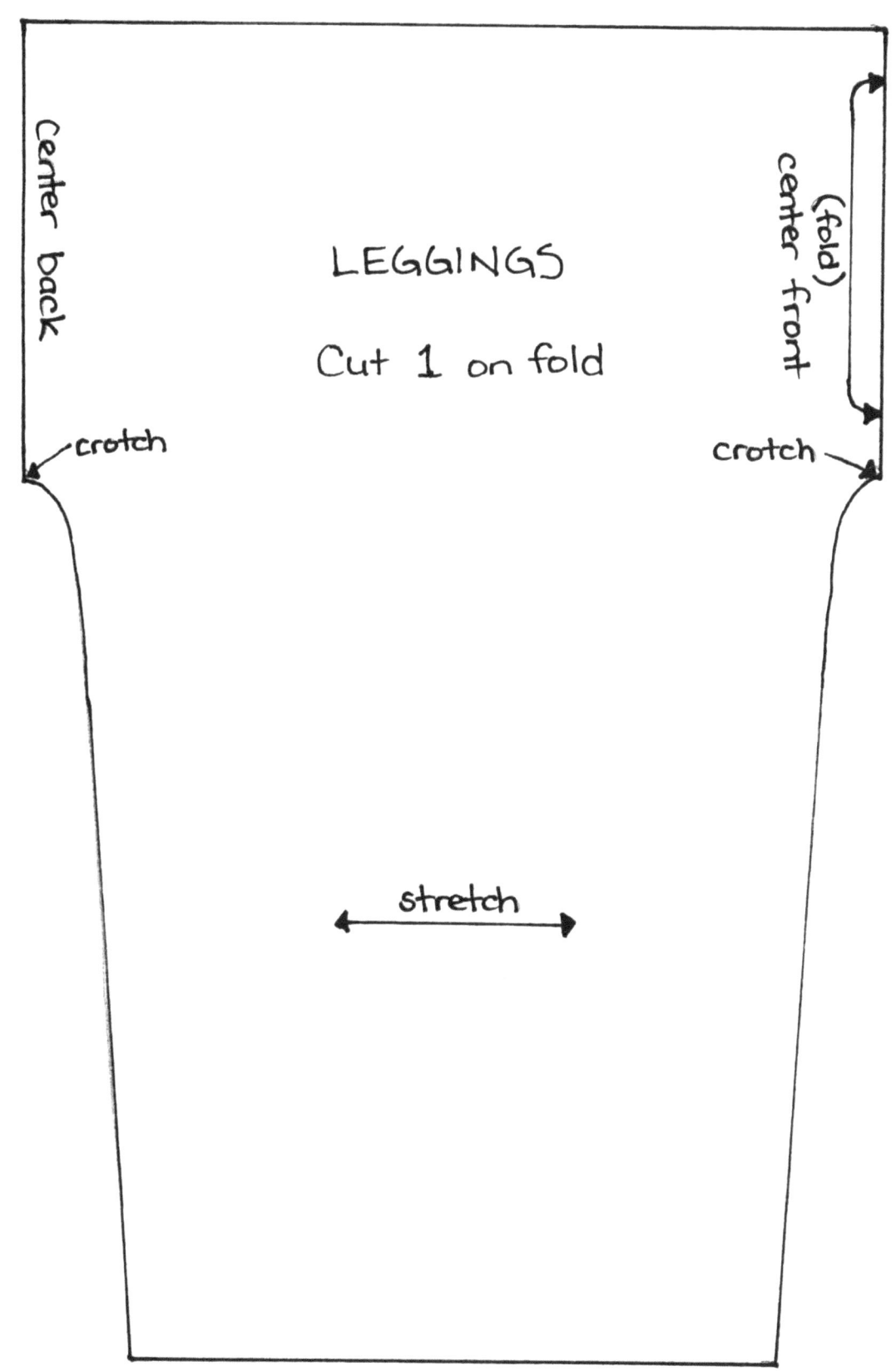

Quick photography tips

Why take photos of your doll? First, it's a great bonding experience. Second, you'll want to brag a little. Third, it's a wonderful way to get connected to the online community of BJD collectors. No one gets tired of lovely shots of BJDs!

Here are a few quick and easy photography tips when snapping photos of your doll. Keep in mind that I am not a professional photographer, and these are simply silly tips from my own experience.

Use natural light and a tripod

If you want clear photos, try to use natural lighting and a tripod to get the best possible photos. You can mimic natural light with a light box, but nothing is better than a bright, natural-lit room, in my humble opinion.

A tripod will hold the camera body steady while you shoot the photo. Even better, use a remote while shooting, so you don't run the risk of moving the camera at all.

That being said, there is something nice about candid hand-held shots. If you have good lighting, you can get away with a lot.

Serious editing

Don't, under any circumstances, keep a blurry photo. Zoom in when you're editing, and make sure you have a clear shot. If you don't get any clear photos in a single shoot, you need more light and a tripod.

The Lucky Shot

Don't discount the lucky shot. One wonderful thing about digital photography is that you can take a lot of photos and then discard all of the blurry ones. I snap a lot of candids (especially when hand-holding), and keep perhaps one out of 50 photos.

Color correct before uploading

Every digital camera has color issues. You'll want to color correct a little bit before uploading your photos to the web, even if it's just using the "enhance" button.

What's your style?

Develop a *style*. Your photos don't have to look like everyone else's. In fact, you should develop your own style, and your photos will have their own unique look. Personally, I like to shoot, according to my husband, like a photojournalist. My style is fun and casual, and I don't like my dolls to look too real or too perfect. I like expressive, pretty pictures with a little bit of glamour or silliness.

Oh, yes. I hand-hold. I know; I just broke one of my own rules. (Come on! You know they aren't rules! They are *suggestions*!)

Read the manual

I know, I know. My husband's camera manual is a thousand pages. And no, I'm not all the way through, either. But really, if you want to take good pictures, you should know your camera.

Further reading

I've included couple of helpful books I've read (for people not really gifted in photography, and not very nerdy about it, like me) in the Resources section.

Joining the BJD Community

Both online and in person, hanging around other BJD collectors is a must, especially for those new to the hobby. Many times, I have found other collectors open to sharing knowledge --little tricks and secrets they have learned throughout the years on how to get the eyes right, or the best way to keep a wig from slipping--just for the sake of getting a new collector excited and encouraged about ball-jointed dolls.

In my experience, you can learn a lot from online message groups and forums, but the best way to learn is from doll meets. You might think you are the only person within 1000 miles who has ever heard of BJDs, or that you are the very oldest collector in the world (or the very youngest). You won't know until you attend a meet.

How do you find meets in your area? It's easiest to find one online, so let's get you connected to the online community first!

Do get connected to the community! It's a great way to find out more information, and get great deals on BJDs!

Netiquette

Just a brief note on online etiquette before we jump into this arena. Manners count when joining any community, including online communities. Before you make your first post, you need to be aware of the following rules of online message forums:

1. Writing responses or posts in ALL CAPS means you are yelling. Don't do it, unless you are putting an emphasis on a single word or using an abbreviation.

    Don't *post off-topic on a message board or forum. Such behavior can be reason to get you booted off the board.*

2. Be familiar with commonly used abbreviations, such as LOL (laugh out loud), DH (dear husband), n00b (pronounced "newb," and meaning newbie), ROFL or ROFLMAS (rolling on the floor laughing my ass off). If you find others you don't understand, look them up online, or use my handy list in the **Common Abbreviations** list.

3. Tone is difficult for people to communicate when writing. Keep this in mind when reading other people's posts, and when you write your own posts, too. Read your post first to make sure it won't offend anyone before clicking that Submit button.

4. Be polite, and follow the golden rule. Generally speaking, would you enjoy reading a post like the one you are writing? Is it adding to the discussion? Is it on-topic and relevant? If you can answer yes to all of these questions, then go ahead and post it.

For specific message groups or boards, consider the following before posting:

1. Read the forum topic rules. Are you posting on-topic? Some boards, like Den of Angels, have a list of BJDs that are considered on-topic, and the others may not be discussed. Your first post should be on-topic.

2. Second, make sure you're posting in the right place. Is there a thread already started for your question or comment? Reply to it, rather than starting an entirely new thread. Search the forum to see if there is already a thread about your topic.

3. Make sure your profile is up to date and follows the guidelines. For instance, make sure your signature follows the rules (you may not be allowed to post for-sale items in your signature, or links to outside sites, for example).

I've found each message board has its own tone. Some can be positive, some are a little negative, some are exclusive, some feel inclusive, and some vary extensively because of the sheer number of users.

You will find lots of helpful information from these online sources--tips, techniques, owner photos, and new release information. I encourage all newcomers to find a board they enjoy. Don't be intimidated by the number of users.

Making online connections

Photo hosting sites

First, you'll need a place on the web to store your best photos of your new favorite beauty. There are many services that you can purchase, but if you aren't a professional photographer, my advice is to save your money (for a new BJD, wig, outfit or eyes) and use a free one.

When you sign up, be sure to read all the terms of service. Some photo hosting services, like Flickr, require that you rate your photos as "safe," "moderate," or "unsafe" before you open them up to the outside world. This is because there are members under eighteen who might be able to see your pictures. Some of their mothers might be offended by photos of a naked doll's breasts, which you have blushed realistically.

Also, be sure you know that your photos can and will be used on the various hosting sites before you upload. Even if you don't allow others to use them, and the terms of service state you retain the rights to your uploaded content, someone still might use it for his or her own purpose.

Why do you need a photo hosting site? Most message boards don't provide photo hosting, so the board requires that you link to the photo's "static link" when you want to share a photo.

Flickr

I recommend Flickr for BJD collectors because of the variety of dolls you will find there. Its easy-to-use interface and gallery function are great for organizing wish lists. You can leave and receive feedback on your photos (or turn this function off, if you prefer). It's a free service for a limited number of photos, and you can upload unlimited photos if you buy a Pro account.

Setting up an account is easy. You sign in with a Google or Yahoo! account and follow the instructions. You control who can see or comment on your photos. If you'd like others to be able to search your photos, use tags. Additionally, you can import contacts from Mail, Yahoo!, Gmail, or Hotmail accounts.

This is how you can post your share your photos on a message forum:

1. From the **You** menu, find the photo you'd like to share.

2. Next to the **Actions** drop down box, click on the **down arrow**.

3. Most message forums (like Den of Angels) use BBCode. Select the **BBCode** radio button, and the size of image you'd like to use.

4. Copy the code in the box, and paste it into your forum message.

5. The code includes a link back to your Flickr page, as required by the Flickr's Community Guidelines.

If your message forum doesn't use BBCode, try the HTML option. You can also find the static URL embedded in this code as well.

Picasa

Picasa is Google's image hosting site. It's easy to use, and it's also free. The interface is intuitive. Simply follow the instructions, or download the uploader.

To add images to a message forum, follow these steps:

1. Find the image you want in the album, and click on it.
2. On the right, click on **Link to this Photo**.
3. Next, under **Embed image**, choose the size you'd like.
4. Now, choose **Image only (no link)**.
5. And copy the URL listed in the **Embed image** box.

> *Do take the time to set up the right photo hosting site for your photos. Make me a contact if you're on Flickr!*

Photobucket

Photobucket is another free image hosting site, but I don't have an account there. The reason I don't use this service is because of what's in the terms of agreement here, in article 6.1:

By displaying or publishing ("posting") any Content on or through the Photobucket Services, **you hereby grant to Photobucket and other users a non-exclusive, fully paid and royalty-free, worldwide, limited license to use, modify, delete from, add to, publicly perform, publicly display, reproduce and translate such Content**, including without limitation distributing part or all of the Site in any media formats through any media channels, except Content marked "private" will not be distributed outside the Photobucket Services. Photobucket and/or other Users may copy, print or display publicly available Content outside of the Photobucket Services, including without limitation, via the Site or third party websites or applications (for example, services allowing Users to order prints of Content or t-shirts and similar items containing Content). [emphasis mine]

Basically, when you upload your photos to this service, you're giving up your right to your own photos, and allowing both Photobucket and private users to do whatever they like with them.

Flickr and Picasa both allow you, the copyright holder, to maintain your rights with your uploaded content.

Online groups

There are a lot of BJD groups available for you to join on Yahoo! Groups. Some are doll-specific, some are region specific, and some are flexible. Here is a list you may consider:

Group	Description
allbjdswelcomehere	Friendly group open to all BJDs.
AmazingBJDDolls	All dolls are welcome. Sales OK on Sunday, but no links to eBay sales.
AmericanBJD	Collectors of American BJDs. No eBay sales or personal doll sales allowed, but signature links for your patterns and clothes are OK.
Angell-Studio	Group for fans of Angell Studio BJDs
AngelOfDream	Group dedicated to Angel of Dream BJDs
angelsoflife	Group dedicated to Ceberus Project dolls and Luts BJDs. This is a UK-based group, I believe.
animalBJDs	Group dedicated to anthro BJDs
balljointeddollymakers	If you're interested in creating your own BJD, check this group out.
BJDsForWomenOfACertainAge	I think the name of the group describes itself!
COBJD	Colorado BJD collectors
Creating_Patterns_for_BJDs	Group dedicated to those who create patterns for BJDs
CreedyCreations	Berdine Creedy's group. No sales allowed.
CreepyOldFolksWhoPlaywDolls	For BJD collectors over the age of 40. Dolls must be resin and ball-jointed. Any place of origin.
DollENews	Denver Doll Emporium's newsletter. They carry BJDs in stock, among other dolls. No sales allowed.
dollfiedream	Primarily focused on Volks Dollfie Dream (vinyl), this group welcomes all BJD collectors.
elfdoll_unlimited	A group dedicated to Rainman's sculpts, produced by Elfdoll
gardenofdolls	Group dedicated to the Garden of Dolls BJD company
Happily	Happily Ever After's newsletter. A dealer which carries American BJDs, Bishonen House and more.
LasherBJDs	Kim Lasher's group. No sales posts allowed, but there is a wish-list database.
Little_Flowers_MSD	Group dedicated to Mini BJDs
LittlewondersBJD	For all tiny Asian BJDs (and they mean LITTLE tinies)
ntexasbjdcollectors	Especially for BJD collectors who live in north Texas.
OurMiniatureDollfies	I'm sure they mean Our Miniature BJDs. ;) It's a group dedicated to the tiniest of tinies.
OurSilentFriends	Discussion group for Japanese and Korean BJDs
Ryung-Sooah	Group dedicated to Rainman's Ryung and Sooah sculpts (Elfdoll)
Sewing_for_BJDs	Group dedicated to those who like to sew for BJDs.
SouthernCalifABJDs	Southern California group dedicated to Asian BJDs. Local meet-ups are scheduled here, and sales posts are allowed.
supiadolls	Group dedicated to Supia Doll from Korea. No sales posts.
Sweetheartsdolls	Sweetheart's Dolls is a dealer which carries some American BJDs, and lots of other fashion dolls.
tristate_angels	New York, New Jersey and Connecticut BJD owners, this group is for you!
westernpabjds	Western PA (Pittsburgh locals) discussing meet-ups and chatting about BJDs.

To join any of these groups, simply type the following into your browser:

http://www.groups.yahoo.com/GROUPNAME/join

Replace GROUPNAME with one of the names above, and follow the instructions. Be sure to read all the group rules and agree to them--especially about posting on-topic and about sales posts--before you make your first post.

Other online resources

Google

Do you need a Google account? Technically, no. But if you join a lot of message boards and forums, you may want an email solely for use with your doll hobby. Plus, a Google account allows you to post on blogs more easily. I recommend it. You can also forward mail from your Google account to another address.

Yahoo!

If you're a fan of Yahoo! groups, you'll more than likely already have a Yahoo! account. You might choose to use this email address instead of your regular address for your doll hobby to help control the information flow.

Facebook

Do you already have a Facebook account? If you do, here are some pages you might find interesting (just add www.facebook.com to the URL links below):

Facebook Page	Description
home.php?sk=group_160631873968967	All BJDs Welcome Here convention
pages/Berdine-Creedy/105134082859238	Berdine Creedy's company page
profile.php?id=100000547523585	BJD Convention - Central CA
profile.php?id=100000089986518	BJD Convention site - Texas 2012
pages/Ball-Jointed-Dolls-BJD/67004721332	BJD fan page
dollwhy	DollWhy's company page - clothing & accessories
pages/The-Fashion-Doll-Review/142781762409712	Fashion Doll Review's fan page
pages/FEATHERFALL-BJDs/101917616524187	Featherfall, a Canadian company's Facebook page
pages/BJDmagazine/103999759668766	Free online magazine for the BJD community
pages/Goodreau-Doll-LLC/63054859992	Goodreau Doll LLC's company page
jennygreydesigns	JennyGrey's company page

If you don't have a Facebook account, I wouldn't highly recommend it; I hypocritically consider Facebook the nation's great time waster. However, I do have a fan page for my blog, The Fashion Doll Review, and we've gotten quite a few new readers this way.

Be careful when friends post links to your page that ask you to share your Facebook information with other sites. There are many sites that "phish" for your password and profile information, your email address and more, masquerading as a Facebook applications.

***Do** be wary of connecting your accounts with outside application that require password sharing!*

Online forums

Message forums, like groups, are almost always run by private individuals. Those individuals take the time to set them up, host them, moderate them, remove spam posts, deal with fraudulent buyers and sellers, and more. For all intents and purposes, the forums belong to those individuals and the moderators who work for them.

You are merely a visitor to the forum, and you agree to follow their rules when you enter. The rules might include:

- No sales outside the marketplace

- No advertising

- No bumping your post (Bring Up My Post: commenting on your own post to bring it to the top of the discussion thread)

- No cross-posting (meaning, posting in the appropriate area, only once)

- No signature or small signature, or limits as to what you may have in your signature

- Discussion on only "on-topic" dolls, which may seem arbitrary to you, but keep in mind: *it's not your board*

- No flaming (meaning, inflammatory posts for the sake of provoking other members)

Keep in mind that some boards have a lighter or more strict tone than other boards, and that every board has a reason for why it does what it does. If you don't think the rules are fair, remember *it isn't your board*, and perhaps you should post somewhere else.

Zone of Zen

This message board is for Asian BJD sculpts only. You must participate in the message forum before you can post items for sale or for auction, and be sure to label any not work-safe or nudity posts appropriately. No "feelers" are permitted on this forum--that is, your doll is either for sale, or it isn't. Your for-sale photos must be your own, and must include proof-of-ownership. This board has its own feedback forum as well.

It's an open and friendly place--the first time I posted I actually received comments within a few minutes. The smaller feel of the forum is definitely less intimidating than some of the other larger forums available.

The dolls that are on-topic at this forum are Asian-style resin ball-jointed dolls. They must be strung with elastic, and have a customizable face. They must have removable eyes and wigs.

According to the rules on Zone of Zen, you must be an "active participant on the board" before making your first sales post. I'm not sure what this means, but I would bet you shouldn't make your initial post (or one of your initial week's postings) a for-sale post. Join the discussions. Get to know the board first, and then sell.

The Resin Cafe

This board is hosted by Kaye Wiggs, maker of KazeKids BJDs. It's a warm and friendly board, open to all BJD enthusiasts. It tends towards a family-friendly atmosphere, and both American and Asian sculpts are allowed on this board.

In the marketplace forum, "feelers" are not allowed--again meaning your doll is either for sale or it isn't. If you list an item for sale, it must be in your hands, and not just on order. Your for-sale posts must include a photo with the item and a note with your name and the date the photo was taken, as proof that the item is in your hands.

Also, you must have at least 30 relevant posts before posting any for-sale items.

American BJDs forum

This is a friendly, easy-going forum originally started by Kim Lasher. Discussion topics originally started for American-sculpted BJDs, but other dolls are welcomed, too. It's a friendly place.

Marketplace access is granted immediately, but the board isn't always active.

Den of Angels

Den of Angels is the largest English-speaking forum on ball-jointed dolls on the web. This group has over 31,000 members, and you need an invitation to join. Members may only send seven invitations per week. If you need an invitation, leave a comment in the BJD section on Fashion Doll Review blog.

This board is divided up into several sections, and you should look around carefully before posting. The News forum is not for chatting; in fact, you might consider only reading the News forum, and letting doll companies do the posting.

> **Do** take the time to find the message board that is the right fit for you. There is one out there!

The discussion section is arranged into General, Large, Mini, Tiny and Anthro dolls. Within each of those sections, you can do a search for the brand of doll you're interested in and find individual discussion threads. You'll notice only one photo per post is allowed in the discussion area.

In order to gain Marketplace privileges, you must have 40 relevant posts and have been an active member for at least 25 days. You will be granted limited access first. After six months and 100 posts, full Marketplace access permits you to start new threads in group orders, splits, original manufacturing, and the commissionable services subforums. Sales on Den of Angels are for on-topic dolls only.

It can be intimidating to post at first. There is a newbie section just for newcomers to Den of Angels and to BJDs. This is the perfect place to start posting and asking questions if you're new to BJDs and Den of Angels.

Introduce yourself--there's an introduction forum--and see around if there might be anyone else in your neighborhood.

Do you know something about styling wigs, or sewing? Post in the customization or sewing section. That's a great way to get started.

Photos are also a great way to get started on Den of Angels. All collectors enjoy viewing beautiful photos of BJDs, as long as they are on-topic.

In the general discussion section, you'll find local doll meet ups. See if you can find one in your area. If there isn't one, why not set one up? You just need room--maybe in a library, for instance--and if you'd like food, have everyone bring a potluck dish to share. You might be able to meet some new people, too. You can make it themed, but give everyone at least a month to prepare.

Meeting BJD collectors in person

Once you've found some people in your area, there are a couple of things you need to know before you attend your first meet or club. Are you nervous? Here are some helpful things to keep in mind when preparing for your first real-life encounter with other collectors:

- You'll probably look like a newbie, but that's OK. Everyone was a newbie once.

- It's normal to be nervous. Whenever you meet people you don't know, it's fine to get a little nervous. The more you see them, the easier it will be.

- There will be a variety of people there. Some may be strange, but others will be perfectly normal and nice. That's just the law of averages.

- You might be the oldest (or youngest) person there. Don't let that bother you.

- You might ask a dumb question, but so did a lot of other collectors when they first started. So don't feel badly, and don't let that stop you from asking questions.

- You probably will see dolls in person that look very different from promotional photos. Dolls look different online than in person.

- Pronunciation is a whole 'nother story. I am *still* not sure whether Iplehouse is Eye-plehouse or Eee-plehouse or Ip-plehouse. My rule of thumb is I try not to say it first, or I ask the owner.

With this in mind, your meet should go off without a hitch. Some other tips you should know about spending time in person with other collectors:

- Don't insult another person's doll. She may not be your type, but I bet her owner thinks she's fabulous. Be positive, not insulting. Do unto others!

- Don't touch another person's doll without asking first.

- Be careful about the price question. Not all BJD owners are comfortable discussing how much money they spent on a doll. Instead, find out the brand and model of the doll, look it up yourself when you get home.

- Don't insult the face-up attempt on a person's doll. It's hard to paint a face-up, and a person who is learning knows whether the attempt is any good or not.

- Don't give advice unless someone asks for it. If you do, it's best to say, "I read this in a book..." or even better, "I read this in Alison Rasmussen's book..."

- It's polite to ask before taking a photo of someone's doll, if the owner is standing there. If you aren't sure of the manufacturer and sculpt, just ask. Most people are typically happy to talk about their dolls.

- Keep in mind that you can enjoy BJDs that aren't on your wish list and that don't fit in with your collection style. Sometimes going to a doll meet can turn your wish list upside down!

- Be social. Even if you aren't usually outgoing, it's ok to ask another owner about how a doll poses, or another how she gets her doll's wig to stay on so well, when you're at a BJD meet.

If you're setting up the meet, you need to determine the rules before the event. Things you might consider:

- Are children allowed? Must they be accompanied by a parent?

- Will food be served? Be sure it is *far* from the dolls so no terrible accidents will happen. Reconsider barbecue sauce, hot wings and delicious guacamole.

- Outdoor meets: do you have a back-up plan in case of rain? Is there shade to protect your dolls from sun?

- Are sales allowed? Will you (or the retailers) need a sales permit?

- Photos: let your attendees know both attendees and their dolls may be photographed, and some of these photos may be uploaded to the web.

- I'd suggest the following rule: Don't touch another person's doll without his or her expressed permission.

- If the meet is at someone's house--are there pets? This allows allergy sufferers to prepare.

BJD collectors, like the rest of the world, come in all shapes, sizes, colors and walks of life. You can learn something from beginners and ancient collectors alike.

While it can be intimidating to *be* a new collector, most experienced BJD enthusiasts are excited to see newbies because they remember when they were brand new to the hobby, too. There is a lot of new information, and so many more dolls available today than even five years ago.

Don't *forget to attend conventions in your area, and support your local doll shops and dealers!*

Conventions

You may think I'm joking about attending a BJD convention, but I'm not. It's a great place to go and meet people, like yourself, who collect ball-jointed dolls.

Depending on the size of the convention, you will find sales tables, often with clothing, wigs, eyes, and sometimes even dolls you can take home with you, right there. At any rate, even if you can't find a doll you like, it's a great place to meet people and see new styles and doll companies.

Most conventions offer tutorials or workshops you can take, in which you will learn a new technique or two. I have shown you a lot in this book, but some people feel more comfortable seeing restringing in person before they are willing to try.

I recommend saving your vacation money to attend a BJD convention. There is one in Austin, Texas every year or so, and one in the Bay area called the GoGa convention. You can find out more details on various message boards, Facebook, and Yahoo! groups.

BJD resources

Here is a handy list of resources you may find helpful in your new hobby. These are companies and resources from which I've used products for my book.

Websites

American BJD Forum	americanbjds.forumotion.com
BJD Collectasy	www.bjdcollectasy.com
Boutique Doll (US DollHeart representative)	www.boutiquedoll.com
Den of Angels	www.denofangels.com
Denver Doll Emporium	www.denverdoll.com
DollHeart	www.dollheart.com
The DollPage	www.dollpage.com
Doll Community Feedback Forum	dollcommunityfeedbackboard.yuku.com
Fashion Doll Review	www.fashiondollreview.com
FroggyDuds	www.froggyduds.com
GingerLime Designs	http://tinyurl.com/gingerlime
JennyGrey Designs	http://jennygrey.etsy.com
Junkyspot	www.junkyspot.com
Kathie's Fashion Dolls	http://stores.ebay.com/Kathies-Fashion-Dolls
Kemper Dolls	www.kemperdolls.com
Mint on Card	www.mintoncardinc.com
Peak's Woods	www.peakswoods.com
The Resin Café	www.theresincafe.proboards.com
Shuga-Shug's Blog	www.shugashug.com
Still Plays With Dolls	www.stillplays.com
Zone of Zen	www.zoneofzen.net

Twitter

Follow The Fashion Doll Review on Twitter: **FDR_alington**

Check out the people we follow and all who follow us. They are a wealth of great information.

Suggested reading

I haven't read many books dedicated to the subject of ball-jointed dolls, but here are some essential resources I've read and enjoyed.

BJD Orbyrarium edited by Aimee Steinberger and Mia Peterson. A magazine-style book with lots of photos, patterns, tutorials and more, many designed for the advanced collector. $25-30 price makes it a bargain.

Designing the Doll: From Concept to Construction by Susanna Oroyan. This book made me want to try making my own doll. $34.95 list price.

Resin Life by Wendy Bailey. A wonderful coffee-table book filled with snapshots of Asian BJDs. $24.95 list price.

Understanding Close-Up Photography by Bryan Peterson. An easy-to-use book on close-up photography, with or without a macro lens. $25.95 list price.

Any photography or Photoshop book by Scott Kelby. They are easy to read and easy to use--I don't use PhotoShop anymore--I use Mac's built-in photo software, iPhoto--but I still use the stuff I learned from Mr. Kelby's books.

Fashion Doll Review

Please check out the links on www.bjdsforbeginners.com for other helpful reading. I wanted to list all of them here, but because of limited space--and the changing nature of the web--I thought an online list would be much more helpful. These are the ones I relied on most in writing my book and learning about BJDs myself!

Photo credits

Cover photo: Normal skin Lavin in DollHeart's Vampire Bride and DollHeart wig.

1-2: White skin Viyol with The Glamour face-up. Outfit by GingerLime Designs, headband by JennyGrey Designs. Acrylic eyes by Kemper Doll. Earrings from Claire's. Peak's Woods wig.

3-4 Normal skin Lavin, in Vampire Bride by DollHeart. Dollheart wigs, eyes by Mint on Card.

5-6: Normal skin Segi in a Rococo gown hand sewn by Katie Brown, altered by JennyGrey Designs. Wig by DollHeart. Eyes by Glib.

7: Tan Briana (The Glamour LE) dressed in Pinky Alice by DollHeart. Wig is part of this set. Eyes from Kemper Dolls.

9-10: Normal skin Lottie Real on FOB body. Nightie by Tonner Doll (Dreams of Tomorrow from the DeeAnna Denton line). Wig by Volks, eyes default. Earrings by me. Lottie is holding a vintage Dawn doll, dressed in an outfit by Pixiedust Designs (Clochette on Den of Angels).

11: Normal skin Goldie in default wig and eyes. Dress and necklace by me. White skin Sky with older default face-up in Leeke wig, default eyes, and outfit by Nancie of Nankatts. White skin Wake-Up Cue in default wig and acrylic eyes by Glib. Pure Red outfit by DollHeart.

15: FOF normal skin Naomi. Glass eyes by Mint on Card, Leekeworld wig. White Fer by DollHeart.

17-18: White skin Skiya with limited edition 2010 face-up. Wig by DollHeart. Hat by Tonner Doll Company. Redingote by Katie Brown, altered by JennyGrey Designs. Silk skirt by JennyGrey Designs.

19-20: Normal skin Minties: Default raven wig, brown glass eyes. Feather eyelashes. Brown wavy wig is Val Zeitler, produced by DollHeart. Outfits by JennyGrey Designs.

21-22: Normal skin Goldie in violet acrylic eyes by Glib and default wig. Outfit by Val Zeitler, produced by DollHeart.

23-24: Normal skin Yulli with default brown acrylic eyes and DollHeart wig and shoes. Outfit by GingerLime Designs.

25: Tan Briana (The Glamour LE) in mohair wig by Michele Hardy and default eyes. Outfit by me.

26: Limited edition full-set Skiya (Christmas event 2010) in her default wig, eyes and outfit.

27: White skin Sky in a wig by Michele Hardy. Outfit by JennyGrey, necklace by Kate Rasmussen.

31: FOB normal skin Morimoth with face-up by Overnight Flight. Monique wig and default acrylic eyes. Outfit by JennyGrey Designs.

32: FOB Lady Bee normal skin head hybrid on a SoulDoll white skin double body. Wig by Kemper, eyes default. Outfit by me.

33-34: White skin LE Wake-Up Lottie Real and normal skin Lottie Real on FOB bodies. Default Peak's Woods wigs and eyes. Outfits by JennyGrey Designs.

35: Normal skin Yeru with default brown acrylic eyes and Monique Gold wig.

35-36: Normal skin Yeru in default wig and blue glass eyes by Volks. Dress by GingerLime Designs.

37: LE Claudine Belmont (Goldie with "bitten" torso) by Peak's Woods, DollHeart and Val Zeitler. Default glass eyes, wig by DollHeart. The Duchess outfit by DollHeart.

38: LE Sonja (Wake-Up Goldie) by Peak's Woods, DollHeart and Val Zeitler. Default glass eyes, DollHeart wig. Renske outfit by DollHeart.

39: Normal skin Goldie with factory face-up, DollHeart wig, violet glass eyes, and outfit by Jenny Grey Designs.

39: White skin Goldie with face-up by Leah Lilly of Froggy Duds. Dark violet eyes by Mint on Card. Wig and outfit (Under the Boardwalk) by Val Zeitler designs by DollHeart.

40: LE Claudine Belmont by Peak's Woods, DollHeart and Val Zeitler. Default glass eyes. The Duchess outfit and wig by DollHeart.

41: Normal skin Mintie with eyes from Mint on Card.

42: White skin Sky with glass eyes in light green from Mint on Card, wig by DollHeart. Outfit by JennyGrey Designs.

43-44: Normal skin Mintie with feather eyelashes and glass eyes. Mohair wig by Kemper. Outfit by Katie Brown, altered by JennyGrey Designs.

45: Normal skin Goldie with default eyes and wig. Dressed in DollHeart's Love 'n the Ice outfit.

46: Normal skin Goldie with glass eyes by Mint on Card, wig by Leeke. Outfit is Under the Boardwalk by Val Zeitler, produced by DollHeart.

47: FOB normal skin Lady Bee, default eyes. Blue wig Monique Gold. Pink wig by Kemper Dolls.

48: FOB normal skin Lady Bee hybrid. Wig by DollHeart, eyes brown acrylic by Kemper. Outfit by Tonner Doll Company. (It's a very snug fit.)

49: Normal skin Segi with glass eyes by Mint on Card and wig by DollHeart. Duchess by DollHeart.

50: Normal skin Yeru the Soul with glass eyes and a wig by DollHeart. Rococo style gown is called Christine, and is manufactured by DollHeart.

51: Normal skin Yeru the Soul on FOB body with default eyes and wig. She's dressed in Dreams of Tomorrow nightie by Tonner Doll Company.

52: Normal skin Yeru the Soul on FOB body and DollHeart wig. Outfit by Michele Hardy.

53: White skin Wake-Up Cue in DollHeart wig. Rococo gown by Soda Clothing for BJDs.

54: Sonja (white skin Wake-Up Goldie) in DollHeart wig and Black Fer. Glass eyes by Mint on Card.

55-56: White skin Wake-Up Lottie on an FOB body is wearing her default eyes and a Val Zeitler wig by DollHeart. Outfit by JennyGrey Designs.

58: Normal skin Lottie Real on an FOB body is wearing her default eyes and an outfit by JennyGrey Designs. The wig is by Volks.

60: Normal skin Mintie in her default eyes and a Monique Gold wig. Red rose fairy outfit by me.

61-62: All photos on these pages were taken by Mark Rasmussen. Model is normal skin Mintie in her default wig. Outfit by JennyGrey Designs.

64: Model is FOB Lady Bee in Tonner Doll outfit.

67-68: Model is normal skin Mintie. Eyes are default acrylic and brown glass.

69: White skin Viyol with The Glamour face-up in default wig and JennyGrey outfit. Earrings by Claire's. Acrylic eyes are by Kemper.

70-72: Normal skin Goldie is wearing a DollHeart wig and outfit by JennyGrey.

87-88: All photos on this page were taken by Mark Rasmussen. Model is normal skin Mintie. Outfit by JennyGrey Designs.

89: Model is Sonja (white skin Wake-Up Goldie).

93-96: Model is normal skin Mintie.

98: Normal skin Segi in Val Zeitler wig and outfit by JennyGrey Designs.

103-104: White skin Hucky is a limited edition full-set Christmas event doll. Her ears are magnetic.

105-106: Claudine Belmont (white skin Goldie) in her default glass eyes and DollHeart wig. Her outfit is by JennyGrey. Shoes by DollZone. La Boutique purse.

107-108: Tan Briana (The Glamour LE doll) in her default eyes and Pouf wig by Val Zeitler, produced by DollHeart. Outfit by JennyGrey Designs.

109-110: Normal skin Yeru in blonde ponytail wig by Volks, brown acrylic eyes. Slightly yellowed white skin Yeru in blonde mohair wig by Kemper and violet glass eyes. Yeru the Soul in golden DollHeart wig and aqua acrylic eyes. All outfits by JennyGrey Designs.

111: FOF Christmas event white skin Hucky full-set in a DollHeart wig. Normal skin Naomi in a vintage Tami playsuit and Peak's Woods wig.

112: Full set limited edition Lavin, normal skin and default eyes. Lutz wig.

113: Normal skin Lavin in fantasy glass eyes and mohair wig by Kemper. Outfit by JennyGrey Designs.

115-116: Christmas event LE Skiya in blue glass eyes and wig by Kemper. Outfit is Vampire Wedding by DollHeart.

117-118: Normal skin Mintie in Val Zeitler wig (by DollHeart) and Kemper acrylic eyes. Outfit by JennyGrey Designs.

119: White skin Briana with a face-up by Overnight Flight. Brown acrylic eyes by Kemper and default Peak's Woods wig. Outfit by JennyGrey designs.

120: White skin Cue with custom face-up by Peak's Woods (using pinks and purples). Glass eyes by Mint on Card (purple) and wig by Monique Gold. Outfit is Tweedle Dum by Val Zeitler, produced by DollHeart.

121-122: A startled normal skin Yulli in giant kelly green glass eyes by Mint on Card. Wig by Luts. Outfit by JennyGrey Designs.

123: White skin Viyol with The Glamour face-up by Peak's Woods. Default wig and dark violet glass eyes by Mint on Card. OOAK bubble dress and earrings by me.

124: White skin Yami with vampire face-up option by Peak's Woods. Default wig and red glass eyes. Yami is wearing Renske by DollHeart.

Doll emergencies

Turn to this section for advice on the most common doll emergencies.

The long winter

Why is my order taking so long? It's been six weeks!

Six weeks is still within the average delivery time frame. In fact, 30-45 days might actually be "working days." Relax. Post a question on the doll company's message board, if you like. Keep in mind, your doll isn't produced until your lay-away payments are completed.

Seriously, it's been a long time.

Go to the Waiting Room area in Den of Angels and see who else is waiting. Are orders arriving? If it's more than a month past the quoted date, contact the company.

My doll arrived; now what?

After all this waiting, and my doll has finally arrived, I don't really want her anymore.

Has your aesthetic changed? Was she an impulse purchase? Do you remember why you ordered her in the first place? If not, put her up for sale. Consider secondary market dolls until you can decide on an aesthetic.

I opened my dream doll, and I hate her. She's not at all like the promotional photos. I'm so disappointed.

Can you change her eyes or wig? Sometimes if the eyes are set incorrectly, it ruins her look. Imagine a different face-up, more natural or dramatic? If you can't imagine ever liking her--if her ears or nose are wrong--then resell. Figure out what happened. Did you see enough real-life photos?

My doll just arrived! I love her! What should I do next?

Start with sanding seam lines, if needed. Fix any stringing problems (though most dolls come strung correctly from the company). Then, blush her if desired, and add sueding, eyelashes, and a manicure.

My brand new dream BJD arrived after three months, and her hand is broken!

First, contact the company and let them know. More than likely, they will replace the hand for you. You won't have to restring completely--just remove the broken part, clamp the elastic with hemostats, and slip a chopstick in the elastic loop. Then, replace the hand.

My brand new doll just lost her foot! I mean, it's totally broken. The elastic is just gone!

Let me guess--it's an Iplehouse, right? (Just kidding!) Chances are, your doll has resin hooks instead of wire. The hands and feet carry the most tension, since that's where the elastic is hooked. Iplehouse uses resin hooks, and they break easily. Replacement parts are available. Remove the leg pieces--it may take some effort, since the broken resin may be stuck in the canal--and then restring the leg with a pipe cleaner or a stringing tool. Hold the elastic loop with a chopstick and carefully hook on the new foot.

My brand new doll will not stand up or hold a pose. She just flops around everywhere. I'm afraid she needs restringing.

You're probably right, especially if you bought a Bobobie, which are known for being strung loosely. First try sueding, and see if that helps. You could also try pulling the elastic up from the neck joint, but if the arms are swingy, too, you probably should restring with a larger diameter elastic.

My doll creeps out my boyfriend/husband/family/dog/cat.

Tell them to grow up. First, it's your money. Second, it's just a doll. Third, it's your new hobby. You'll probably get another one. Leave the doll in conspicuous places, posed in helpful positions, like folding the laundry. Well, don't scare the dog or cat. That could be hazardous.

My doll creeps me out.

What? I think you may be in the wrong hobby. Go post your doll for sale at half price on eBay or something, or send it to me as payment for my helpful advice.

Help, I just broke my doll!

I was removing the head cap and the magnets just fell off.

Go to page 65 for a tutorial on how to glue them back on.

My doll fell onto the floor and broke a finger. She's ruined!

If you still have the finger piece, you can glue it back on using the same technique as above, or order a replacement hand from the company.

My doll fell onto the floor, and she isn't chipped, but she won't stand up anymore.

She probably broke off a piece from inside her torso. You'll need to remove her head and legs to know for sure, but it can be re-glued.

The replacement piece I ordered from the company doesn't match my doll!

Try blushing the new piece to make the resin match. Make sure to seal it well and suede the joint to keep it from wearing too quickly.

Help, I'm having serious budgeting problems!

I went over my budget this month, and now I have to tell my spouse.

Oh, boy! Lucky you. Don't do it again. You'd better be honest and admit it. Don't "save it for a better time." Don't wait.

I went onto the Marketplace (or eBay) and committed to buy items I don't have the money to buy.

You're going to get negative feedback if you don't follow through on your transactions. If you're on a message board, offer a trade. Otherwise, talk to you spouse. You don't want to be known as a flake. Don't go window shopping if you can't control yourself.

Index

A

abbreviations (see *terminology*)

about this book, 3

acetone, 58, 95-96

advice, 122

aesthetic styles, 23-24, 25-26, 27, 37-40, 49, 67-72

alcohol, for drinking, 81, 84

alcohol, rubbing, 58

Aleene's Fast Grab Tacky Glue, 93-94

Alice in Wonderland, 7, 21-22, 120

American BJDs, 7, 25-26, 116, 118

articulation, 18, 37-38

Asian BJDs, 7, 25-26

B

ball-jointed doll definition, 2, 5-6, 8

ball-jointed doll history, 7

ball-jointed dolls as art, 19, 21

ball-jointed dolls as investment, 18, 19-20

ball-jointed dolls, difference between American and Asian sculpts, 25-26

ball-jointed dolls, difference between fashion dolls, 6, 8, 17, 19-20, 32

ball-jointed dolls, handling, 42, 60, 121

ball-jointed dolls, how to choose, 23-42,

ball-jointed doll proportions, 5, 9, 25, 32

ball-jointed doll sizes, 9, 32, 37, 49, 50, 79

ball-jointed doll terminology, 12-16

ball-jointed doll value, 19, 37-40

basic doll, 17, 39

beginning collectors, 3, 21-22, 99, 123

Bella Dark, 39

Berdine Creedy, 7, 26, 114

Biscardi, Jacquie, see *GingerLime Designs*

blushing (see *body blushing*)

BJD Collectasy, 2, 125

Bobobie, 7, 12, 14, 78, 131

body blushing 12, 76, 89-90

body types 7, 17, 32, 38, 40, 51

Boutique Doll, see *DollHeart*

Briana by Peak's Woods, 7, 25, 107-108, 119

Brown, Katie, 5-6, 17-18, 23, 43-44

brushing (see *body blushing*)

broken dolls, 3, 47, 65-66, 75-76, 83, 130-131

budgeting, 3, 20, 22, 35-36, 44-44, 131

buying BJDs (see *purchasing BJDs*)

C

caution, 21-22, 35, 78, 86, 87, 112, 121-123

Cerberus Project, 7

chalk, 57, 89-90

changing eyes, 67-68

Chinese New Year, 18, 36

children and BJDs, 8

Cholong, Ms., see *DollHeart*

cleaning resin, 58, 60-61

clothing and shoes, 51, 98-99

collecting BJDs, 19-20, 21-22, 24, 44

colored resin, 47-48, 75

community, 105-106

companies, 28-31

company feedback and reputation, 18, 45, 51

contact the author, 3

conventions, 124

copies (see *knock offs*)

cosplay, 12

crazy legs, 73

Cue by Peak's Woods, 120

customization, 19-20, 40, 50, 89-90, 91-92, 93-94

Custom House, 7

D

Dawn by Ideal, 8-9

dealers, 50

DeeAnna Denton, 8-9

definition of ball jointed doll (see *ball-jointed doll definition*)

delivery time, 18, 45, 130

Den of Angels, 2, 18, 23, 36, 45, 51, 108, 119-120

dents, 75-76

Denver Doll Emporium, 12, 114, 125

de-yellowing resin, 95-96

doll clothing (see *clothing*)

Dollfie, 12

DollHeart, cover, 3-4, 5-6, 7, 11, 17-18, 19-20, 21-22, 23-24, 37-38, 39-40, 42, 45, 48, 53-54, 52, 53, 70-72, 105-106, 107-108, 109-110, 111, 115-116, 117-118, 124

Dollovely, 63, 73

Dollmore, 8, 12, 14, 29

Dollpage Show & Sell, 45, 52, 125

Dollzone, 7, 13, 29, 106

Doll in Mind, 7, 12, 28

double-jointed, 12, 26, 38

Duchess, The, 37, 40, 49

Dullcote, Testors 56, 57

Dust of Dolls, 12, 32

E

eBay, 7, 16, 44, 45, 52, 114, 130

elastic, 5, 14, 64, 79, 80, 98-99

Elfdoll, 13, 14, 29, 114

emergenices, 130-131

Enku, Akihiro, 7

Eugley, Jen, see *JennyGrey Designs*

exaggerated features of BJDs, 27, 28-31

eye placement, 37, 69-72

eye sizes, 38, 41, 59, 71-72

eye types, 6, 41, 59, 71-72

eyelashes, 39, 43-44, 61, 93-94

eyes, 6, 38, 41, 59, 67-68

F

Facebook, 4, 115-116, 124

face-up, 6, 17, 39, 41, 48, 51, 61, 122

face-up, removing, 58

Fairyland, 7, 9, 12, 13, 14, 29

Fairy of Color, 9, 50, 59

Fairy of Bugs, 9, 50

Fairy of Fairytales, 9, 50

fantasy dolls, 6, 27, 28-31, 32

family and friends, 21, 131

fashion BJDs, 8, 32

feedback, 18, 48

feeler, 13, 117

Fer, 15, 54

Flickr, 18, 33-34, 110

fragility of resin, 8

French nails, 91-92

FroggyDuds, see *Leah Lilly face-up*

full set, 40

G

GingerLime Designs, 1, 23-24, 35-36, 125

glass eyes, see *eye types*

Glamour face-up by Peak's Woods, 1-2, 7, 25, 107-108, 123

Glib acrylic eyes 1, 5-6, 11, 21-22, 27, 46, 67, 72

Goldie by Peak's Woods, 11, 21-22, 37, 39-40, 45-46, 70-72, 105-106

Goodreau Dolls, 7, 26, 116

Google, 115

H

handmade, 2, 19

Hardy, Michele, 25, 27, 52

Haute Doll exclusive Peak's Woods dolls, 37, 38, 40, 54, 89, 105-106

head, removing your doll's, 77

head, replacing your doll's, 87

head cap, 65-66

history of BJDs (see BJD history)

how to use this book, 3

Hucky by Peak's Woods, 103-104, 111

hybrid dolls, 39, 49

I

insomnia, 22

Iplehouse, 13, 14, 29, 86, 122, 130

J

JennyGrey Designs 1, 5-6, 17-18, 19-20, 23, 27, 31, 33-34, 39, 42, 43-44, 55-56, 59, 62, 70-72, 97, 98-102, 105-106, 107-108, 109-110, 113, 117-118, 119, 121-122

jointing, see *articulation*

Junkyspot, 57, 125

K

Kemper Dolls, 2, 19-20, 32, 43-44, 47, 69, 72, 94, 109-110, 113, 115-116, 117-118

kicky dolls, 73-74, 77-86

Kim Lasher BJDs, 7, 26, 118

knock offs, 7, 18

Kristine, 50

L

La Boutique, 106

Lady Bee by Peak's Woods, 32, 47-48, 64

large BJDs (see *ball-jointed doll sizes*)

Lasher, Kim (see *Kim Lasher BJDs*)

Lavin by Peak's Woods, cover, 3-4, 112, 113

lay-away, 35, 36, 40, 44, 49

Leah Lilly face-up, 39, 125

liking or loving your dolls, 44-45

Lilly, Leah, see *Leah Lilly face-up*

limited edition dolls, 39, 44

limited face-up, 39

Liquitex gloss, 91

Lottie Real by Peak's Woods, 8-9, 33-34, 59

Love 'n the Ice, 45

M

Mack's silicone ear plugs, 65

Magic Eraser, 58, 60, 89-90, 95

magnets, 6, 65-66

maintenance, 60-61

make-up (see *face-up*)

manicure, see *French nails*

meet-ups, 49, 121-123

mini BJDs (see *ball-jointed doll sizes*)

Mini Gem, 9

Mini Super Dollfie, 9

Mint on Card, 3-4, 15, 17-18, 19-20, 39, 41, 46, 49-50, 64, 70-71, 109-110, 113, 115-116, 120, 121-122, 123-124

Mintie by Peak's Woods, 19-20, 41, 43-44, 60, 62, 94, 96

Mr. Superclear, 57, 75-76, 89-90, 96

modifications, 75-76

mohair wigs, see *Hardy, Michele*

moleskin, 60, 63, 73-74

Monique Gold, 31, 35, 47, 60, 120

Morimoth by Peak's Woods, 31

MSC, see Mr. Superclear

MSD (see *Mini Super Dollfie* or *ball-jointed doll sizes*)

N

Nankatts, 11

Naomi by Peak's Woods 15, 111

netiquette, 16, 107-108

O

obsessive behavior, 22, 42

odors, see *smoke smell*

on-topic posting, 108, 115, 117, 119-120

online behavior (see *netiquette*)

organization, 24, 33-36

Overnight Flight face-up, 31, 119

P

PamSD, see *Dollovely*

parting lines (see *seam lines*)

pastels, see *chalk*

payment methods, 51

Peak's Woods, 7, 9, 23, 41, 42, 50, 59

pedicure, see *French nails*

photo hosting services, 109-112

photography, 103-104, 109, 120, 122

Photobucket, 112

Picasa, 111

Pinky Alice, 7

Pixiedust Designs, 9-10

planning your collection, 24, 23-42, 33-36

posing, 18, 26, 37, 73-74

pre-loved BJDs, see *secondary market*

price, 37-38, 47, 51, 52, 122

price and quality, 37-38, 40, 47, 59

production location, 37

purchasing BJDs, 17, 24, 43-52, 48

Pure Red, 11

Q

quality, 17-18, 25-26, 40, 42, 80

R

Rasmussen, Kate, 27

realistic BJDs, 27, 28-31

recast (see *knock offs*)

references, see *feedback*

removing a BJD's head, see *head*

Renske, 38, 124

repairing resin, 8, 36, 95-96

resin 5, 8, 42

resin and metal, 83, 86, 87

Resin Café, The, 18, 118

resin sprays, 55 (see also *Mr. Superclear* and *Dullcote, Testors*)

resin types, 37, 47

resin versus vinyl, 8

resin yellowing (see *yellowing*)

restringing, 77-86

Rococo, 5-6, 17-18, 43-44

rules at meet-ups, 121-123

rules for message forums, 25, 117

S

sanding seam lines, 5, 37, 39, 40, 75-76

scratches, 8, 47, 58, 75-76

sculpting details, 38-39

SD (see *Super Dollfie* or *ball-jointed doll sizes*)

sealing a face-up, 61

seam lines, 5, 26, 39, 40, 75-76

secondary market, 36, 45, 52-53

Segi by Peak's Woods, 5-6, 49, 98

sewing for your doll, 98-99

sewing resources, 99

shipping BJDs, 52-53

shoes, see *clothing and shoes*

silicone ear plugs

Skiya by Peak's Woods, 17-18, 26, 115-116

Sky by Peak's Woods, 11, 42

smoke smell, 36, 44, 52

socket joint, 8, 73

Soda Clothing for BJDs, 53

Soom, 9

Souldoll, SoulKid body, 32

stringing, 5, 46, 77-86,

stylistic preferences, 26

sueding, 73-74

superglue, 65-66

Super Dollfie, 7, 9

supplies for your BJD, 56, 59

Sybarites, 8

T

tan resin, 37, 47

tension, 81, 85

terminology (see *ball-jointed doll terminology*)

teminology, web-specific (see *web-specific terminology*)

Testors Dullcote, see *Dullcote*

tiny dolls (see *ball-jointed doll sizes*)

Tonner Doll Company, 8, 9-10, 17-18, 48, 51, 64

tutorials, 55-104

Tweedle Dee outfit, 21-22, 120

Twitter, 126

U

unstringing, 78

used BJDs, see *secondary market*

UV coating, 37, 57

UV rays, 42, 122

V

Val Zeitler face-ups, 37-38, 105-106

Val Zeitler outfit, 21-22, 46

Val Zeitler wig, 19-20, 39, 55-56, 98, 107-108, 117-118, 120

Vampire Wedding, cover, 3-4, 115-116

vinyl, 8, 91-92

Viyol by Peak's Woods, 1-2, 69, 123

Volks, 7, 9

Volks wigs and eyes, 8-9, 35-36, 59

W

Wake-Up Cue by Peak's Woods, 11, 53

Wake-Up Goldie by Peak's Woods, 36, 54

Wake-Up Lottie by Peak's Woods, 33-34, 55-56

Wake-Up Yeru (see *Yeru the Soul*)

water and resin, 58, 60

watercolor pencils, 91

web-specific terminology, 16

where to buy BJDs, 49-53

Wiggs, Kaye, 26, 118

wig cap, 63

wig fixes, 63-64

wig measurement, 41

wig placement, 41, 60-61

wig sizes, 6, 41, 59, 64

window shopping, 33-34

Winsor & Newton's Brush Cleaner, 58

wish list, 33-36

Y

Yami by Peak's Woods, 124

Yahoo!, 115

Yahoo! Groups, 114

yellowing, 26, 37, 42, 47, 95-96

Yeru by Peak's Woods, 35-36, 109-110

Yeru the Soul by Peak's Woods, 50, 51-52

Yoon, Eugene, see *Overnight Flight*

YoSD (see also *ball-jointed doll sizes*), 9

Yulli by Peak's Woods, 23-24, 121-122

Z

Zeitler, Val, see *Val Zeitler* and *Haute Doll exclusives*

Zone of Zen, 18, 117-118

www.ingramcontent.com/pod-product-compliance
Lightning Source LLC
Chambersburg PA
CBHW041549220426
43666CB00002B/16